Insights into the Therapeutic Applications of Fasting

Edited by Cristina Manuela Drăgoi, Ion-Bogdan Dumitrescu, Anca Ungurianu and Alina Crenguta Nicolae

Published in London, United Kingdom

Insights into the Therapeutic Applications of Fasting
http://dx.doi.org/10.5772/10.5772/intechopen.1004993
Edited by Cristina Manuela Drăgoi, Ion-Bogdan Dumitrescu, Anca Ungurianu and Alina Crenguta Nicolae

Contributors
Alina Crenguţa Nicolae, Anca Ungurianu, Ankita Kondhalkar, Ashish Anjankar, Cristina Manuela Drăgoi, Ferdinando Franzoni, Giorgia Scarfò, Ion-Bogdan Dumitrescu, Jonathan Fusi, Linda Afriyie Gyimah, Mohd Basheeruddin, Rakesh Kumar Jha, Robin Mesnage, Sana Qausain, Ying Yang

First published in London, United Kingdom, 2025 by IntechOpen
IntechOpen is the global imprint of INTECHOPEN LIMITED, registered in England and Wales, registration number: 11086078, 167-169 Great Portland Street, London, W1W 5PF, United Kingdom

For EU product safety concerns: IN TECH d.o.o., Prolaz Marije Krucifikse Kozulić 3, 51000 Rijeka, Croatia, info@intechopen.com or visit our website at intechopen.com.

British Library Cataloguing-in-Publication Data
A catalogue record for this book is available from the British Library

Insights into the Therapeutic Applications of Fasting
Edited by Cristina Manuela Drăgoi, Ion-Bogdan Dumitrescu, Anca Ungurianu and Alina Crenguta Nicolae
p. cm.

This title is part of the Food Science and Nutrition Book Series, Volume 12
Topic: Nutrition
Series Editor: Maria Rosário Bronze
Topic Editors: Simon Welham and Peter Rose

Print ISBN 978-0-85014-871-8
Online ISBN 978-0-85014-870-1
eBook (PDF) ISBN 978-0-85014-872-5
ISSN 2977-8174

IntechOpen Book Series

Food Science and Nutrition

Volume 12

Aims and Scope of the Series

The significance of food is undeniable, especially in light of the impending challenge facing humanity: ensuring there will be enough food to meet the basic needs of a population expected to reach approximately 10 billion by 2050. These food-related challenges align with some of the United Nations' sustainable development goals, with a target to achieve them by 2030. One thing is certain: food should be not only nourishing and safe but also tailored to the diverse needs of individuals throughout their lifetimes, all while meeting consumers' sensory expectations. Understanding the diverse chemical composition of food, often referred to as biodiversity, and how these components can contribute to human health by considering factors like bioaccessibility, bioavailability, and bioactivity at the organ level, is crucial for grasping and promoting a healthy diet. Thanks to the continuous evolution of analytical methods and interdisciplinary research, significant strides have been made in the field of food science and nutrition.

Meet the Series Editor

Maria Rosário Bronze has been working in Analytical Chemistry since 1986. Her Ph.D. in 1999 contributed to the study of food products using capillary electrophoresis. The main goal of her research since 1999 has been focused on Analytical Chemistry applied mainly to the analysis of foods and by-products of food industry. She conducted research in collaboration with national and international research groups, at iBET and ITQB Technology Division. From 2017 until 2021 she was head of Food & Health Division at iBET and head of the Food Functionality and Bioactives Laboratory. MR Bronze has been an Associate Professor at the Pharmacy Faculty of Lisbon University and head of the Structural Analysis Laboratory since 2012. As a researcher, MR Bronze is a Senior Scientific Advisor at Food & Health Division at iBET and Head of Food Functionality and Bioactives Laboratory at the same Institute, Collaborator at iMED and Researcher at ITQB NOVA. Her current research is focused on quality and beneficial health effects of food components. Gas and liquid chromatography associated with mass spectrometry are used by MR Bronze in the characterization of samples. Sensory evaluation is also an important area of her research. The main food products studied by her are olive tree products (olive, olive oil, leaves), cereals such as maize, legumes (faba bean, pea, chickpea, lentils) fruits (apple, grapes, opuntia ficus), fruit juices and wine, among others. More recently her interests have also involved biodiversity, bioaccessibility, and bioavailability studies on food products and their components, mainly phytochemicals as phenolic compounds, using different analytical tools such as mass spectrometry. As a senior scientific advisor at Food & Health Division at iBET she is involved in different areas: (i) isolation, characterization and formulation of bioactive and functional compounds or extracts from natural sources and wastes from food and other related industries; (ii) pre-clinical assays to provide support to understand health claims related with the beneficial effects of food nutrients/bioactive components; (iii) establishment of analytical methodologies including mass spectrometry state-of-the-art to fully characterize different matrices, from food products, natural extracts or biological fluids (Food Functionality and Bioactives Laboratory).

Meet the Volume Editors

Cristina Manuela Drăgoi, Ph.D., is a pharmacist and associate professor at the Department of Biochemistry, Faculty of Pharmacy, University of Medicine and Pharmacy "Carol Davila", Bucharest, Romania. She has professional experience in oxidative stress mechanisms, assessing drugs' effects on biochemical markers and identifying predictive biomarkers for metabolic diseases. Her scientific research focuses on revealing circadian entrainment actions on major physiological and pathological processes, determining its modulatory abilities on different aspects of hormone synthesis, healthy ageing mechanisms and nutrition and medicines administration. This captivating subject of applied biochemistry in drug research is the core of her scientific projects, a fact also depicted by her authorship of several books, book chapters and research articles.

Ion-Bogdan Dumitrescu, Ph.D., joined the Physics and Informatics Department of the Pharmacy Faculty, Carol Davila University of Medicine and Pharmacy in Bucharest, Romania, in 2007, where he currently holds an Associate Professor position. His doctoral thesis involved research on bio-relevant in vitro release conditions for low-soluble pharmaceutical compounds. His main research interest revolves around 3D printing applied for pharmaceutical preparations, though many other collaborations have arisen in the past few years. He also conducted research in the field of chronobiology and circadian rhythms. His experience allowed him to publish several research articles, books and book chapters on a wide range of health aspects, enabling a better understanding of the circadian governance of human life at different levels.

Anca Ungurianu, Ph.D., is a Lecturer in the Department of Biochemistry, Faculty of Pharmacy, University of Medicine and Pharmacy "Carol Davila", Bucharest, Romania.

Her doctoral studies focused on the development and optimization of accessible and high-throughput methods of assessing redox imbalances in serum- and tissue-derived samples, the resulting set of biomarkers being useful in both preclinical and clinical inflammation-related experimental settings. Currently, her postdoctoral studies focus on the effects of key metabolites of some of the best-known polyphenols/related natural compounds on members of the sirtuin family, enzymes reported to regulate numerous physiological processes with important links to chronobiology and circadian rhythms. She contributed to the expanding research field of inflammatory, metabolic, and ageing-related diseases through several important publications, articles, and book chapters.

Alina Crenguța Nicolae, Ph.D., is an associate professor at the Department of Biochemistry, Faculty of Pharmacy, University of Medicine and Pharmacy "Carol Davila", Bucharest, Romania. She completed her Ph.D. thesis on biochemical mechanisms involved in multidrug resistance, this subject remaining one of the major pillars of her activity. She is passionate about the field of neuropharmacology. Her research projects conducted so far focus on the individual neuro-biochemical profile, correlated with age, gender, race, metabolic and genetic profiles, as well as the establishment of predictive biomarkers that trigger the response to pharmacotherapy and multidrug resistance mechanisms modulation at the level of the blood-brain barrier. Mrs. Nicolae is a pharmacist specialized in clinical pharmacology, a field encompassing drug properties, functions, sources, synthesis and drug design, molecular and cellular mechanisms, signal transduction and cellular communication, molecular diagnostics, interactions, chemical biology, therapy, medical applications, and antipathogenic capabilities.

Contents

Preface

Fasting and caloric restriction regimens have proven their beneficial effects on health and lifespan and their potential application in managing chronic metabolic diseases, acquiring increasing attention from the medical perspective due to their therapeutic benefits beyond traditional religious or cultural contexts. This interest has led to extensive research aimed at understanding the physiological, biochemical, and clinical implications of fasting on human health. For various fasting regimens, ranging from intermittent fasting, where individuals alternate between periods of eating and fasting, to prolonged fasting lasting several days or more, clinical research has revealed profound effects on metabolism, cellular processes, and overall health.

The book *Insights into the Therapeutic Applications of Fasting* intends to explore the multifaceted aspects of fasting through a comprehensive examination of scientific literature and clinical studies, aiming to elucidate the mechanisms underlying the therapeutic potential of fasting and explore its applications in various medical conditions. Our journey begins with an overview of the physiological responses to fasting, including changes in metabolism, hormone regulation, and cellular repair mechanisms. We continue with emerging evidence supporting the use of fasting as a therapeutic intervention for a range of health conditions, including obesity, type 2 diabetes, cardiovascular disease, and cancer.

Furthermore, we plan to highlight the potential role of fasting in promoting longevity and cognitive function, as well as its impact on immune function, inflammation, and gut health. Throughout the book, we provide insights into the efficacy, safety, and practical considerations surrounding fasting as a medical intervention.

By synthesizing current knowledge and perspectives on fasting from diverse fields of study, this book aims to contribute to a deeper understanding of its therapeutic applications and update healthcare professionals about its potential benefits and limitations, and nevertheless to foster informed discussions and further research into the role of fasting in promoting human health and well-being.

Cristina Manuela Drăgoi, Anca Ungurianu, Ion-Bogdan Dumitrescu and Alina Crenguța Nicolae
'Carol Davila' University of Medicine and Pharmacy,
Bucharest, Romania

Chapter 1

Introductory Chapter: Insights into the Therapeutic Applications of Fasting

Cristina Manuela Drăgoi, Anca Ungurianu, Ion-Bogdan Dumitrescu and Alina Crenguța Nicolae

1. Introduction

Fasting, a practice rooted in ancient traditions and diverse cultures, has garnered significant attention in modern biomedical research for its profound implications on human health. Fasting is now recognized as a potent physiological intervention with applications spanning exercise science, immunology, cellular health, and the management of chronic diseases.

Fasting induces a cascade of biochemical and physiological changes that extend beyond simple caloric restriction. At its core, fasting triggers a metabolic switch from glucose to lipid utilization, a process mediated by the depletion of glycogen reserves in the liver and subsequent activation of lipolysis. This shift leads to the production of ketone bodies, such as beta-hydroxybutyrate (BHB), which serves as an alternative energy source for peripheral tissues, including the brain. Ketone bodies not only provide fuel but also exert anti-inflammatory and neuroprotective effects by modulating signaling pathways such as nuclear factor kappa B (NF-κB) and NF-E2-related factor-2 (Nrf2), thereby reducing oxidative stress. Simultaneously, fasting stimulates mitochondrial biogenesis and enhances electron transport chain efficiency, leading to improved cellular energy production and reduced generation of reactive oxygen species (ROS), key contributors to oxidative damage and aging [1–3].

The hormonal adaptations associated with fasting are equally critical. Levels of insulin decrease, enhancing insulin sensitivity and facilitating the mobilization of stored energy. Concurrently, glucagon and growth hormone levels rise, promoting gluconeogenesis and lipolysis. These hormonal shifts also influence leptin and ghrelin, hormones responsible for appetite regulation, creating a feedback loop that supports energy balance, and prevents overeating. Enhanced activity of the AMP-activated protein kinase (AMPK) and mammalian target of rapamycin (mTOR) pathways further reinforces cellular energy homeostasis, promoting catabolic processes during fasting and anabolic recovery during refeeding. These mechanisms mitigate metabolic disturbances commonly associated with insulin resistance and type 2 diabetes while promoting metabolic flexibility [4, 5].

One area of significant interest is the interplay between fasting and physical performance. During fasting, the reliance on fat oxidation increases, sparing muscle glycogen and improving endurance in certain contexts. Furthermore, fasting-induced increases in mitochondrial biogenesis and enhanced fatty acid metabolism contribute to improved energy efficiency. Studies suggest that fasting can upregulate peroxisome proliferator-activated receptor-gamma coactivator 1-alpha (PGC-1α), a key regulator of mitochondrial function and adaptation to exercise. However, the timing and duration of fasting relative to exercise are crucial variables, as prolonged fasting may activate proteolytic pathways *via* the ubiquitin-proteasome system, leading to protein catabolism and reduced performance in high-intensity activities. Tailored fasting strategies are therefore essential for athletes to optimize both performance and recovery [6, 7].

The immune system also experiences profound modulation during fasting. A key mechanism is the reduction in circulating pro-inflammatory cytokines, such as interleukin-6 (IL-6) and tumor necrosis factor-alpha (TNF-α), and an increase in anti-inflammatory mediators. Fasting induces a transient reduction in white blood cell counts, followed by a rejuvenation of hematopoietic stem cells upon refeeding, a process mediated by the insulin-like growth factor I (IGF-I) and protein kinase A (PKA) signaling pathways. These effects suggest a potential role for fasting in enhancing immune resilience and improving outcomes in conditions such as chronic inflammation and autoimmunity. Emerging evidence also links fasting to the modulation of gut microbiota composition, fostering microbial diversity and reducing dysbiosis, which plays a critical role in immune system regulation [8, 9].

In the context of chronic diseases, fasting has demonstrated considerable potential in addressing cardio-metabolic disorders. It enhances insulin sensitivity through the AMPK signaling pathway and improves lipid profiles by reducing triglycerides and LDL cholesterol. Furthermore, fasting promotes weight loss, primarily from visceral fat stores, reducing the risk of metabolic syndrome. These effects underscore fasting's role as a multifaceted intervention for conditions such as obesity, hypertension, and type 2 diabetes. Additional studies highlight fasting's influence on endothelial function, with improved nitric oxide availability and vascular reactivity, factors critical in cardiovascular health [10].

At the cellular level, fasting is a powerful inducer of autophagy, a lysosomal degradation pathway critical for maintaining cellular homeostasis. By recycling damaged organelles and proteins, autophagy mitigates cellular stress and prevents the accumulation of toxic aggregates implicated in neurodegenerative diseases such as Alzheimer's and Parkinson's. Moreover, fasting-induced autophagy has been linked to improved mitochondrial function and reduced cancer cell proliferation, highlighting its relevance in aging and oncology. Research demonstrates that fasting can modulate key regulators of autophagy, including Beclin-1 and microtubule-associated protein 1A/1B-light chain 3 (LC3), which facilitates the formation of autophagosomes, and the inhibition of mTOR, which serves as a central autophagy suppressor. This intricate interplay ensures cellular renewal and longevity. By reducing IGF-1 levels and inhibiting anabolic pathways such as mTOR, fasting creates a metabolic environment that is less conducive to cancer cell proliferation. Moreover, fasting may enhance the efficacy of chemotherapy and radiotherapy by sensitizing cancer cells while protecting normal cells through differential stress resistance [11–13].

For aging, fasting offers a holistic approach to extending health span—the period of life spent in good health. Through the activation of sirtuins, FOXO transcription factors, and other longevity pathways, fasting reduces oxidative stress, enhances DNA repair, and promotes mitochondrial biogenesis. These molecular changes not only delay the onset of age-related diseases but also improve overall physiological resilience [14].

Despite its benefits, fasting is not without risks, particularly for individuals with underlying health conditions or advanced age. Prolonged fasting can lead to nutritional deficiencies, as the intake of essential vitamins, minerals, and amino acids is significantly reduced. Such deficiencies can impair immune function, compromise bone health, and exacerbate existing chronic conditions.

Another concern is the potential for muscle loss during extended fasting. While short-term fasting primarily utilizes fat stores for energy, prolonged fasting can activate proteolytic pathways, leading to the breakdown of muscle proteins for gluconeogenesis. This poses a significant risk for older adults, who are already at increased risk of sarcopenia and frailty [15–17].

In individuals with diabetes, fasting may precipitate hypoglycemia, particularly if medications such as insulin or sulfonylureas are not adjusted. Hypoglycemia can have severe consequences, including cognitive impairment, cardiovascular complications, and in extreme cases, coma. Careful medical supervision is therefore essential when implementing fasting protocols in this population [18].

Fasting can also have psychological impacts. For individuals with a history of eating disorders, fasting may exacerbate unhealthy behaviors or trigger relapses. Additionally, the initial phases of fasting, characterized by hunger, irritability, and fatigue, can affect mental clarity and productivity, posing challenges for those with demanding lifestyles. Cardiovascular risks, though less common, must also be considered. Prolonged fasting can lead to electrolyte imbalances and dehydration, which may increase the risk of arrhythmias and orthostatic hypotension. These risks are particularly relevant for individuals with pre-existing heart conditions or those on diuretic medications [19].

Finally, improper refeeding following a fasting period can negate its benefits. Overeating or consuming high-glycemic foods during refeeding may lead to weight cycling, a phenomenon associated with increased cardiovascular risk and metabolic dysfunction.

2. Fasting: A balanced perspective

Fasting, whether intermittent, time-restricted, or prolonged, modulates multiple molecular pathways, offering potential benefits in the management of chronic diseases and the mitigation of age-related physiological decline. However, its clinical implementation must be carefully evaluated to balance its benefits against potential risks, particularly in vulnerable populations.

Fasting represents a double-edged sword, with the potential to significantly improve health outcomes while posing risks if not implemented judiciously. Its benefits, spanning improved metabolic health, reduced inflammation, enhanced autophagy, and delayed aging, are underpinned by robust biochemical mechanisms that offer exciting opportunities for therapeutic applications. However, its risks, including nutritional deficiencies, hypoglycemia, and psychological impacts, necessitate a personalized approach to its adoption.

The integration of fasting into medical practice through evidence-based protocols and interdisciplinary collaboration is the way forward. By leveraging advancements in biomarker research, wearable technologies, and patient education, fasting can be tailored to individual needs, maximizing its benefits while minimizing its risks. With continued research, fasting holds the promise of transforming how we approach chronic diseases and aging, offering a scientifically grounded path toward enhanced health and longevity [20–24].

The book, *Insights into the Therapeutic Applications of Fasting*, presents a multidisciplinary examination of fasting, bridging the gap between foundational science and clinical practice.

Author details

Cristina Manuela Drăgoi*, Anca Ungurianu, Ion-Bogdan Dumitrescu and Alina Crenguța Nicolae
"Carol Davila" University of Medicine and Pharmacy, Bucharest, Romania

*Address all correspondence to: manuela.dragoi@gmail.com

References

[1] Hoddy KK et al. Intermittent fasting and metabolic health: From religious fast to time-restricted feeding. Obesity (Silver Spring). 2020;**28** (Suppl. 1):S29-S37

[2] Tang D et al. Fasting: From physiology to pathology. Advanced Science (Weinheim, Baden-Württemberg, Germany). 2023;**10**(9):e2204487

[3] Zairi I et al. Effect of intermittent fasting and chronotherapy on blood pressure control in hypertensive patients during Ramadan. Arterial Hypertension. 2022;**26**(2):67-72

[4] Patterson RE, Sears DD. Metabolic effects of intermittent fasting. Annual Review of Nutrition. 2017;**37**:371-393

[5] Ooi T et al. Antioxidant potential, DNA damage, inflammation, glycemic control and lipid metabolism alteration: A mediation analysis of Islamic Sunnah intermittent fasting on cognitive function among older adults with mild cognitive impairment. The Journal of Nutrition, Health & Aging. 2022;**26**(3):272-281

[6] Doherty R, Madigan S, Warrington G, Ellis J. Sleep and Nutrition Interactions: Implications for Athletes. Nutrients. 11 Apr 2019;**11**(4):822. DOI: 10.3390/nu11040822

[7] Drăgoi CM, Dumitrescu I-B, Nicolae AC. Introductory chapter: Untangling the essential links among the circadian rhythm, homeostasis of the human body, and the nutritional, behavioural, and pathological interferences. In: Circadian Rhythm-New Insights into Physiological and Pathological Implications. London, UK: IntechOpen; 2022

[8] Flanagan A et al. Chrono-nutrition: From molecular and neuronal mechanisms to human epidemiology and timed feeding patterns. Journal of Neurochemistry. 2021;**157**(1):53-72

[9] Frank J et al. Brain–gut–microbiome interactions and intermittent fasting in obesity. Nutrients. 2021;**13**(584):2021

[10] Nicolae AC et al. Chronotherapy advances in the management of chronic neurological and cardiovascular diseases: Complex interactions of circadian rhythm environmental inputs, nutrition and drug administration and their impact on human health. In: Circadian Rhythm-New Insights into Physiological and Pathological Implications. London, UK: IntechOpen; 2022

[11] Ayyar VS, Sukumaran S. Circadian rhythms: Influence on physiology, pharmacology, and therapeutic interventions. Journal of Pharmacokinetics and Pharmacodynamics. 2021;**48**(3): 321-338

[12] Dong TA et al. Intermittent fasting: A heart healthy dietary pattern? The American Journal of Medicine. 2020;**133**(8):901-907

[13] Arora N et al. Intermittent fasting with ketogenic diet: A combination approach for management of chronic diseases. Clinical Nutrition ESPEN. 2023;**54**:166-174

[14] Lee MB et al. Antiaging diets: Separating fact from fiction. Science. 2021;**374**(6570):eabe7365

[15] Barbu CG et al. Cardiovascular risk assessment in osteoporotic patients using osteoprotegerin as a reliable predictive

biochemical marker. Molecular Medicine Reports. 2017;**16**(5):6059-6067

[16] Drăgoi CM, Nicolae AC. Introductory chapter: Melatonin, the integrative molecule within the human architecture. In: Melatonin-Molecular Biology, Clinical and Pharmaceutical Approaches. London, UK: IntechOpen; 2018

[17] Chai R et al. Circadian rhythm in cardiovascular diseases: A bibliometric analysis of the past, present, and future. European Journal of Medical Research. 2023;**28**(1):194

[18] Yang M et al. Intermittent fasting—A healthy dietary pattern for diabetic nephropathy. Nutrients. 2022;**14**(19):3995

[19] Malinowski B et al. Intermittent fasting in cardiovascular disorders—An overview. Nutrients. 2019;**11**(3):673

[20] Allada R, Bass J. Circadian mechanisms in medicine. New England Journal of Medicine. 2021;**384**(6):550-561

[21] Franzago M et al. Chrono-nutrition: Circadian rhythm and personalized nutrition. International Journal of Molecular Sciences. 2023;**24**(3):2571

[22] Drăgoi C, Moroşan E, Dumitrescu I-B, Nicolae AC, Arsene AL, Drăgănescu D, et al. Insights into chrononutrition: The innermost interplay amongst nutrition, metabolism and the circadian clock, in the context of epigenetic reprogramming. Farmacia. 2019;**67**:4. DOI: 10.31925/farmacia.2019.4.2

[23] Patikorn C et al. Intermittent fasting and obesity-related health outcomes: An umbrella review of meta-analyses of randomized clinical trials. JAMA Network Open. 2021;**4**(12):e2139558

[24] Almoosawi S et al. Chronotype: Implications for epidemiologic studies on chrono-nutrition and cardiometabolic health. Advances in Nutrition. 2019;**10**(1):30-42

Chapter 2

Fasting Physiological Effects

Linda Afriyie Gyimah

Abstract

Fasting is a widespread practice across cultures and religions, involving abstaining from food and sometimes specific types of food for defined periods. Fasting has evolved into a ritualistic, spiritual, and health-promoting practice. Fasting encourages the body to create ketones. These molecules act as a substitute energy source for different body parts, with the brain particularly proficient at utilizing them for energy. This cascade of metabolic adaptations involves several key organ systems: the pancreas for hormonal regulation, the liver for glycogen storage and fat metabolism, adipose tissue as an energy reserve, and skeletal muscle as a potential protein source—all working in concert to maintain energy homeostasis during periods of fasting. Fasting can positively impact various markers of health, including cardiovascular disease, cancer, and neurodegenerative diseases. While highlighting potential benefits, the review also acknowledges potential negative effects as well. This review summarizes the literature on fasting and its effects on the body.

Keywords: fasting, ketosis, gluconeogenesis, autophagy, gut microbiome, insulin sensitivity

1. Introduction

Throughout the past and across diverse societies and faiths, people have engaged in fasting. Historically, fasting has been associated with spiritual purification and religious observance [1]. In contemporary settings, fasting is also adopted for weight management, metabolic health improvements, and potential therapeutic benefits in chronic disease prevention and treatment [2]. Fasting is a means of refraining from consuming any food or beverage for a specified duration. In a broader interpretation, it may also involve avoiding particular types of food for a set period of time [3]. Fasting is the abstinence from all or some foods or drinks for a set period of time. Fasting, the voluntary abstinence from food for a period of time, induces various physiological effects in the human body. These effects may be positive or negative. Normally, most human beings engage in an unintentional overnight fast between 8 and 12 hours daily. In the early days, humans fasted inadvertently when they were not certain about the safety of foods. As human culture developed, fasting became associated with religious devotion, often performed as a sacrifice to deities. Additionally, fasting is seen as a method to purify both the physical body and the mind [4]. The physiological effects of fasting are orchestrated by complex interactions among various organ systems, hormonal signaling pathways, and metabolic adaptations. Delving into metabolic shifts, hormone regulation, and cellular repair processes, this topic sheds light on how fasting influences health, longevity, and overall well-being. As human societies progressed, fasting became associated with multiple purposes:

1. Religious devotion: Many faiths (Christianity, Islam, and Judaism) incorporate fasting as a spiritual practice or offering to deities.

2. Physical well-being: Fasting is seen as a way to cleanse and rejuvenate the body.

3. Political expression or protest: Some individuals or groups use fasting as a form of non-violent demonstration.

4. Medical reasons: Prior to surgical operations.

Different mechanisms exist to enable the storage of energy and its mobilization when fasting or during periods of starvation. The following are the mechanisms that exist during fasting based on the duration [5].

1. Fed phase (0–4 hours after eating)

Digestion of recently consumed food and absorption of its nutrients actively occur in this phase. Consequently, blood sugar concentrations increase, triggering the pancreas to secrete insulin. This hormone facilitates cellular absorption of glucose and converts surplus glucose into glycogen, which is then stored in the liver and muscle tissues. When there is a positive energy balance, that is, when caloric intake exceeds immediate energy needs, the excess calories are stored as fat.

2. Postabsorptive phase (4–18 hours)

In this phase, blood sugar begins to decline when the body has completely absorbed the nutrients from the previous meal. To keep blood glucose within a normal range, the body begins to break down glycogen stored in the liver in a process called glycogenolysis. This leads to a decrease in insulin production and a corresponding increase in the secretion of the hormone glucagon. This hormonal shift boosts the release of glucose that had been stored earlier.

3. Gluconeogenesis (18–48 hours)

After the liver's glycogen reserves are exhausted, the body shifts to manufacturing glucose from sources other than carbohydrates in a process termed gluconeogenesis. This process primarily uses amino acids obtained from breaking down proteins. Concurrently, the breakdown of fat (lipolysis) accelerates, which releases fatty acids that can be used as an energy source. This dual approach helps the body maintain its energy needs when carbohydrate sources are no longer available.

4. Ketosis (48–72 hours)

With prolonged fasting, the body substantially accelerates the process of breaking down fat. In the liver, fatty acids are transformed into compounds called ketone bodies (acetoacetate, β-hydroxybutyrate, and acetone). Ketone bodies serve as an alternative fuel source for various organs, with the brain particularly proficient at utilizing them for energy. This metabolic state, characterized by elevated ketone levels in the blood, is referred to as ketosis.

5. Protein conservation (72+ hours)

During extended periods of fasting, the body implements strategies to protect muscle tissue. The rate of protein breakdown decreases as the body adapts to this state. Simultaneously, the body's efficiency in utilizing ketones as an energy source improves. To further safeguard muscle mass, there is an increase in the production of growth hormones. These coordinated changes allow the body to maintain essential muscle tissue while relying primarily on fat-derived energy sources during prolonged fasting.

2. Classification of fasting

Fasting can be classified based on duration, frequency, and the degree of caloric restriction. Thus, fasting may be short-term or prolonged (>8 days). The following are the classifications of fasting:

1. Intermittent fasting

Intermittent fasting (IF) entails consistent, alternating periods of restraint from caloric consumption and ad libitum eating. The three intermittent fasting approaches that have received the most research attention in human studies are alternate-day fasting, the 5:2 method, and time-restricted eating [2]. These three protocols represent the most commonly investigated forms of intermittent fasting in the scientific literature. Each approach offers a different pattern of alternating between periods of normal eating and periods of caloric restriction or complete fasting.

a. Alternate-day fasting (ADF)—with ADF, individuals fast on alternating days, that is, fasting is done for 24 hours and ad libitum eating days the following day.

b. The 5:2 method—this involves fasting for two non-consecutive days per week and 5 days of normal eating.

c. Time-restricted eating—this involves daily fasting for 12–20 hours. Examples are the 16:8 diet, where the individual fasts for 16 hours and eats for 8 hours daily.

2. Religious fasting—various fasting practices are associated with different religions.

a. Christians: Christians observe a 40-day period of fasting and abstinence, excluding Sundays, modeled after Jesus Christ's 40-day fast in the wilderness before he began his public ministry. This practice, often called Lent, involves self-discipline, spiritual reflection, and abstaining from certain foods or activities as a means of spiritual preparation and renewal.

b. Ramadan fasting (Islamic): Ramadan fasting is a month-long Islamic practice where Muslims abstain from food, drink, and other physical needs from dawn to sunset. This period of daily fasting is accompanied by increased prayer, charity, and self-reflection, aiming to strengthen faith and foster spiritual growth. While exempt groups exist, most adult Muslims participate, adjusting their daily routines to accommodate pre-dawn and post-sunset meals.

c. Yom Kippur fasting (Jewish): Yom Kippur, the Day of Atonement, is the holiest day in the Jewish calendar. It involves a 25-hour complete fast from food and drink, starting before sunset on the evening before Yom Kippur and ending after nightfall the next day. This fast is observed by most adult Jews, except those whose health would be at risk. The fasting is part of a broader day of prayer, repentance, and self-reflection, aimed at spiritual cleansing and renewed commitment to Jewish faith and values.

3. Therapeutic fasting—this is used as a medical intervention, often under supervision.

   a. Water fasting: Consumption of only water for a set period, typically for detoxification or weight loss.

   b. Juice fasting: Consumption of only fruit and vegetable juices for a set period

4. Fasting-Mimicking Diets (FMD)—FMD requires strict health expert supervision. It involves the consumption of very-low-calorie diets that aim to produce similar metabolic effects as complete fasting. It typically involves five consecutive days of severe calorie restriction (800–1100 kcal/day) repeated periodically (e.g., once a month).

During fasting, multiple organ systems are affected, with the pancreas playing a primary role in the initial response. As blood glucose levels drop, the pancreas increases glucagon secretion from the alpha cells in the islets of Langerhans. This hormone primarily targets the liver, which houses the majority of the body's glycogen stores, while also affecting skeletal muscle to a lesser degree due to its lower glycogen content.

The pancreas operates independently through its connection to both the sympathetic and parasympathetic nervous systems. Additionally, various parts of the brain, such as the hypothalamus, cerebellum, and hippocampus, contain insulin receptors. These receptors are not limited to these areas but are found in other brain regions as well.

Once hepatic glycogen is depleted, the body shifts to utilizing adipose tissue and proteins for energy. The liver becomes central to fat metabolism, serving as the main site for triglyceride oxidation. In prolonged or extreme fasting situations, when fat sources are exhausted, the body resorts to breaking down skeletal muscle for energy. This process provides amino acids for metabolism but results in a decrease in muscle mass.

When we consume food, the digestive tract releases specific hormones. These gut hormones play crucial roles in regulating several physiological processes, including the following:

1. Control of appetite

2. Regulation of glucose production

3. Management of gastric emptying rates

4. Facilitation of glucose uptake from the bloodstream

These hormones act as key mediators in the body's response to nutrient intake, helping to maintain metabolic balance and energy homeostasis.

This cascade of metabolic adaptations involves several key organ systems—the pancreas for hormonal regulation, the liver for glycogen storage and fat metabolism, adipose tissue as an energy reserve, and skeletal muscle as a potential protein source—all working in concert to maintain energy homeostasis during periods of fasting [6].

3. Physiological effects of fasting

Fasting triggers a significant shift in how our cells function and how our body processes energy. This change induces various positive or negative physiological effects in the human body, which are discussed below:

3.1 Metabolic effects

Normally, when we eat, the body obtains nutrients from the food for various functions, including energy production. The body relies on glucose in the blood for energy through a process called glycolysis. However, during fasting, the body must maintain blood glucose levels differently. The human body changes from the use of glucose for energy to fat oxidation during fasting. Initially, it taps into glycogen (stored glucose) reserves located in the liver and skeletal muscles. Glycogen consists of linked glucose molecules that can be broken down for energy through glycogenolysis. The liver, which holds the largest glycogen stores, plays a crucial role in sustaining blood glucose levels during the first day of fasting. Once about 24 hours have passed, these glycogen reserves become depleted. At this point, the body shifts to using energy stored in fat tissue and protein sources to maintain its functions [7]. After glycogen stores are exhausted, a major metabolic shift occurs, primarily driven by the breakdown of fat stored in adipose tissue. This process involves the following:

a. Triglyceride breakdown: Triglycerides in fat cells are split into free fatty acids and glycerol.

b. Liver conversion: The liver transforms these components—glycerol is converted to glucose, while free fatty acids are converted to ketone bodies (β-hydroxybutyrate, acetone, and acetoacetate), a process known as ketogenesis for energy use. The production of ketones serves as an alternative energy source for the brain and other organs. The brain, which typically relies heavily on glucose, gradually adapts to use ketones for up to 60–70% of its energy needs during prolonged fasting.

c. Energy distribution: Ketone bodies circulate through the body and are converted back to acetyl-CoA in tissues needing energy.

Simultaneously, protein breakdown (catabolism) occurs through gluconeogenesis. This process creates glucose from amino acids derived from various body tissues, including muscle. This newly created glucose helps maintain blood sugar levels and provides energy for glucose-dependent tissues (like the brain, although the brain can also use ketones to some extent). These simultaneous processes demonstrate how the body adapts to maintain energy balance during fasting, using both fat and protein stores to meet its energy needs. The shift to ketone body utilization helps spare protein by reducing the need for extensive gluconeogenesis, though some protein breakdown still occurs. Mattson et al. [8] describe that this metabolic change can enhance glucose control, boost resilience to stress, and reduce inflammation. The transition to using ketone bodies is linked to elevated levels of brain-derived neurotrophic factor (BDNF), which supports cognitive function and neuroplasticity.

3.2 Insulin sensitivity

Fasting periods allow insulin levels to decrease significantly, giving cells a break from constant exposure to this hormone. This can lead to improved insulin sensitivity, meaning cells become more responsive to insulin when it is present. Additionally, fasting may increase the expression of insulin-sensitive glucose transporters (GLUT4) in muscle cells. This improved insulin sensitivity can lead to better glucose control and potentially reduce the risk of type 2 diabetes [9]. Another study [10] demonstrated that alternate-day fasting for 2 weeks increased insulin-mediated glucose uptake rates by 25%. This improvement in insulin sensitivity can have far-reaching effects, potentially reducing the risk of type 2 diabetes and other metabolic disorders.

3.3 Cardiovascular health

Fasting can positively impact various markers of cardiovascular health. Moro and colleagues [11] studied the effects of time-restricted feeding (16 hours of fasting, 8 hours of feeding) over 8 weeks. They found significant reductions in blood pressure, total cholesterol, low-density lipoprotein (LDL) cholesterol, and triglycerides. Research on intermittent fasting suggests it can significantly improve blood lipid profiles. Studies examining both alternate-day and whole-day fasting protocols, lasting from 3 to 24 weeks, have demonstrated notable reductions in various lipid markers. Participants across different weight categories experienced decreases in LDL cholesterol (20–25%), total cholesterol (5–21%), triglycerides (14–50%), and triacylglycerol concentrations (15–30%) [12, 13]. Additionally, Longo and Mattson [9] found that intermittent or periodic fasting has protective effects against diabetes, cancers, heart disease, and neurodegeneration in rodents, while human studies have alleviated obesity, hypertension, asthma, and rheumatoid arthritis. These consistent findings across multiple studies and fasting methods indicate that intermittent fasting can be an effective approach for lowering blood lipids, which may contribute to improved cardiovascular health, therefore, potentially reducing the risk of cardiovascular diseases.

3.4 Autophagy

Autophagy is a vital cellular maintenance process that utilizes lysosomes to break down and recycle various components within the cell [14]. This mechanism serves as a protective housekeeping system, targeting and eliminating damaged organelles, misfolded proteins that have outlived their usefulness, and even invading pathogens. By recycling these cellular materials, autophagy provides building blocks and energy for cellular renovation and helps maintain homeostasis. This process is crucial for cells to adapt to stress and maintain optimal function. Essentially, autophagy acts as a cellular "self-eating" system that cleans up, recycles, and renews cellular components, thereby promoting overall cellular health and resilience [14]. Enhanced autophagy has been associated with improved neuronal health, reduced inflammation, and better overall cellular function. The activation of autophagy during fasting is thought to be an evolutionary adaptation that allows organisms to recycle cellular components for energy and maintain cellular health during periods of nutrient scarcity [14]. Another study [15] also found out that short-term fasting (24–48 hours) induced a dramatic upregulation of autophagy in brain cells. This increased autophagy may contribute to the neuroprotective effects of fasting, potentially reducing the risk of neurodegenerative diseases.

3.5 Inflammation

Chronic inflammation is associated with numerous diseases, including cardiovascular disease, cancer, and neurodegenerative disorders. Fasting appears to have anti-inflammatory effects. Research [16, 17] indicates that fasting reduces markers of systemic inflammation, such as C-reactive protein (CRP), tumor necrosis factor-α (TNF-α), and interleukin-6 (IL-6). This anti-inflammatory effect may be mediated through several mechanisms, including the reduction of oxidative stress, modulation of the gut microbiome, and alterations in gene expression. The anti-inflammatory effects of fasting may contribute to its potential benefits for various chronic diseases. Fasting appears to increase the vulnerability of cancer cells to chemotherapy while potentially protecting healthy cells, thus reducing side effects [18]. It induces metabolic changes that counter cancer cells' typical adaptations, such as the Warburg effect, and promotes apoptosis in these cells [19, 20], which leads to an increase in oxygen consumption while decreasing adenosine triphosphate (ATP) synthesis, suggesting heightened mitochondrial uncoupling [21].

3.6 Neurological effects

Fasting shows promising neuroprotective effects, potentially enhancing cognitive function and lowering the susceptibility to neurodegenerative diseases. A study [22] demonstrated that intermittent fasting protected against age-related cognitive decline in animal models. The researchers found that fasting reduced neuroinflammation and oxidative stress in the brain, which are key factors in cognitive decline and neurodegenerative diseases.

3.7 Hormonal change

Fasting influences the secretion of various hormones. One notable effect is the increase in human growth hormone (HGH) secretion. A study [23] found that a two-day fast increased the frequency and amplitude of growth hormone secretory bursts in men. HGH plays crucial roles in metabolism, muscle growth, and cellular repair processes. According to Longo and Mattson [9], other hormonal changes during fasting include decreased insulin levels, increased glucagon levels, and increased norepinephrine levels. Insulin levels decrease rapidly, allowing for increased lipolysis and fatty acid oxidation. During fasting periods, increased secretion of glucagon stimulates processes such as glycogenolysis and gluconeogenesis, which help maintain stable blood glucose levels [24]. Growth hormone production is elevated, which helps preserve lean body mass and enhance lipolysis. Norepinephrine levels rise, contributing to increased alertness and potentially boosting basal metabolic rate. These hormonal shifts orchestrate many of the metabolic adaptations observed during fasting and play crucial roles in mobilizing energy stores and maintaining homeostasis in the absence of food intake.

3.8 Gut microbiome

The gut microbiome plays a critical role in overall health, influencing metabolism, immunity, and brain function. Fasting has been shown to significantly impact the composition of the gut microbiome. According to a systematic review [25], intermittent fasting results in an increase in beneficial bacteria, such as Firmicutes, and a decrease in harmful bacteria. These changes are associated with higher production of short-chain fatty acids, which offer various health benefits, including improved gut barrier function and reduced inflammation. Researchers also noted that these microbiome alterations coincide with increased browning of white adipose tissue, potentially enhancing metabolic health and aiding in weight management.

These effects suggest that fasting could contribute to improved health outcomes, such as better metabolic health, reduced inflammation, and enhanced cellular repair processes. However, it is essential to recognize that the effects of fasting can vary depending on the specific fasting regimen, duration, and individual characteristics.

4. Negative effects of fasting

Fasting, whether practiced for religious, weight-loss, or purported health reasons, can have significant adverse effects on the body if not approached cautiously. Again, the desired results may not be obtained if improperly done. For instance, a religious fasting like Ramadan offers valuable insights into brief food restrictions in healthy individuals. Contrary to popular belief, research suggests that Ramadan fasting does not necessarily lead to reduced food consumption. Studies have shown that energy intake either increases or remains steady before, during, and after Ramadan, despite fewer meals being consumed [26, 27]. Other potential negative effects of fasting include nutrient deficiencies, muscle loss, decreased metabolism, and electrolyte imbalances. It is therefore prudent to explore the potential negative effects of fasting as well.

One of the primary concerns is the risk of nutritional deficiencies due to prolonged periods without food, which can lead to inadequate intake of essential vitamins, minerals, and macronutrients [28]. This is particularly concerning for micronutrients that require regular intake, such as water-soluble vitamins. These deficiencies can weaken the immune system, impair cognitive function, and hinder physical performance [29]. In a study investigating adverse events and eating disorder symptoms during alternate day fasting [30], participants reported experiencing constipation in 17% of cases, water retention in 2%, dizziness in less than 20%, and general weakness in less than 15%.

For individuals with certain medical conditions or histories of disordered eating, fasting can exacerbate symptoms or trigger unhealthy behaviors [31]. Muscle loss is also a potential consequence, as the body may break down muscle tissue for energy when calorie intake is insufficient, especially if protein intake is inadequate [9].

Moreover, fasting can disrupt hormonal balance, particularly insulin levels, affecting blood sugar control and potentially increasing the risk of metabolic disorders [2]. Additionally, a study [32] suggests a potential disruption in menstrual cycles in women and affecting fertility due to fasting and dietary restrictions. Fasting also increases the likelihood of hypoglycemia in individuals with type 1 diabetes, posing a notable health concern [33].

Fasting has also been related to impaired cognitive function. Some people experience difficulty concentrating and decreased cognitive performance during fasting periods [34]. In their study on the impact of long-term fasting and intermittent fasting on cognitive abilities, researchers [35] discovered that both types of fasting could potentially impair cognitive function and decrease word production levels. In cases of prolonged fasting, reintroducing food too quickly can lead to refeeding syndrome, a potentially life-threatening condition [36]. Refeeding syndrome is a potentially life-threatening condition that can occur when severely undernourished individuals receive rapid nutritional support, either through tube feeding or intravenous methods. This syndrome is characterized by dangerous fluctuations in fluid balance and electrolyte levels, triggered by the body's hormonal and metabolic responses to sudden nutrient intake. These physiological changes can lead to severe medical complications [36].

It is important to note that the severity and likelihood of these negative effects can vary greatly depending on the individual, the duration and type of fasting, and their overall health status. Many of these risks are more pronounced with extended fasting periods or in individuals with pre-existing health conditions.

Therefore, while fasting may offer benefits when managed appropriately, it is crucial to consult with a healthcare professional, especially for pregnant or lactating mothers, individuals with eating disorder problems, as well as those with chronic health conditions, and approach fasting practices with awareness of potential risks.

5. Conclusion

During fasting, the body undergoes significant metabolic changes aimed at maintaining energy balance. Initially, the pancreas increases glucagon secretion as blood glucose levels drop, prompting the liver to release stored glycogen. Once glycogen reserves are depleted, the body shifts to burning fat and protein for energy. This metabolic switch involves processes like ketogenesis, where fat is converted into ketone bodies that serve as an alternative fuel source, especially for the brain.

Fasting also affects insulin sensitivity positively, potentially reducing the risk of type 2 diabetes. Cardiovascular health may improve, as evidenced by reductions in blood pressure and cholesterol levels. Autophagy, a cellular cleaning process, increases during fasting, promoting cellular health and potentially reducing inflammation.

However, fasting can have negative effects if it is not approached carefully. These include nutrient deficiencies, muscle loss, hormonal imbalances, and impaired cognitive function. Individuals with certain medical conditions or histories of disordered eating should be cautious, as fasting could exacerbate symptoms.

In summary, while fasting offers potential health benefits such as improved metabolism and cardiovascular health, it is essential to consider individual health needs and risks. Consulting with a healthcare professional before starting a fasting regimen is advisable, particularly for vulnerable populations.

Author details

Linda Afriyie Gyimah
Department of Food and Nutrition Education, University of Education, Winneba, Ghana

*Address all correspondence to: lagyimah@uew.edu.gh

References

[1] Venegas-Borsellino C, Sonikpreet, Martindale RG. From religion to secularism: The benefits of fasting. Current Nutrition Reports. 2018;**7**(3):131-138. DOI: 10.1007/S13668-018-0233-2/METRICS

[2] Anton SD et al. Flipping the metabolic switch: Understanding and applying the health benefits of fasting. Obesity. 2018;**26**(2):254-268. DOI: 10.1002/oby.22065

[3] Ganesan K, Habboush Y, Sultan S. Intermittent fasting: The choice for a healthier lifestyle. Cureus. 2018;**10**(7). DOI: 10.7759/CUREUS.2947

[4] Natarajan RSRS, Kannan M, Sathiyarajeswaran P, Gopakumar K, Pandian SJJ. Fasting—A medico historical overview. International Refereed Journal of Reviews and Research. 2018;**2**(1). ISSN 2348-2001

[5] Gordon Betts PDJ, Young KA, Wise JA, Johnson E, Poe B, Kruse DH, et al. Anatomy and Physiology, Nutrition and Metabolism. In: OpenStax. 2nd ed. Houston, Texas; 2022. [Accessed: June 16, 2024]. Available from: https://openstax.org/books/anatomy-and-physiology-2e/pages/24-5-metabolic-states-of-the-body

[6] Nakrani MN, Wineland RH, Anjum F. Physiology, glucose metabolism. In: StatPearls. 2023 [Accessed: July 21, 2024]. Available from: https://www.ncbi.nlm.nih.gov/books/NBK560599/

[7] Browning JD, Baxter J, Satapati S, Burgess SC. The effect of short-term fasting on liver and skeletal muscle lipid, glucose, and energy metabolism in healthy women and men. Journal of Lipid Research. 2012;**53**(3):577-586. DOI: 10.1194/JLR.P020867

[8] Mattson MP, Moehl K, Ghena N, Schmaedick M, Cheng A. Intermittent metabolic switching, neuroplasticity and brain health. Nature Reviews. Neuroscience. 2018;**19**(2):81-94. DOI: 10.1038/nrn.2017.156

[9] Longo VD, Mattson MP. Fasting: Molecular mechanisms and clinical applications. Cell Metabolism. 2014;**19**(2):181-192. DOI: 10.1016/j.cmet.2013.12.008

[10] Halberg N, Henriksen M, Söderhamn N, Stallknecht B, Ploug T, Schjerling P, et al. Effect of intermittent fasting and refeeding on insulin action in healthy men. Journal of Applied Physiology Md. 1985. 2005;**99**(6):2128-2136. DOI: 10.1152/japplphysiol.00683.2005

[11] Moro T et al. Effects of eight weeks of time-restricted feeding (16/8) on basal metabolism, maximal strength, body composition, inflammation, and cardiovascular risk factors in resistance-trained males. Journal of Translational Medicine. 2016;**14**(1):1-10. DOI: 10.1186/S12967-016-1044-0/TABLES/4

[12] Varady KA, Bhutani S, Klempel MC, et al. Alternate day fasting for weight loss in normal weight and overweight subjects: A randomized controlled trial. Nutrition Journal. 2013;**12**:146

[13] Tinsley GM, La Bounty PM. Effects of intermittent fasting on body composition and clinical health markers in humans. Nutrition Reviews. 2015;**73**(10):661-674. DOI: 10.1093/nutrit/nuv041

[14] Bagherniya M, Butler AE, Barreto GE, Sahebkar A. The effect of fasting or calorie restriction on

autophagy induction: A review of the literature. Ageing Research Reviews. 2018;**47**:183-197. DOI: 10.1016/j.arr.2018.08.004

[15] Alirezae M, Kemball CC, Flynn CT, Wood MR, Whitton JL, Kiosses WB. Short-term fasting induces profound neuronal autophagy. Autophagy. 2010;**6**(6):702-710. DOI: 10.4161/auto.6.6.12376

[16] Johnson JB et al. Alternate day calorie restriction improves clinical findings and reduces markers of oxidative stress and inflammation in overweight adults with moderate asthma. Free Radical Biology and Medicine. 2007;**42**(5):665-674. DOI: 10.1016/J.FREERADBIOMED.2006.12.005

[17] Faris MAIE et al. Intermittent fasting during Ramadan attenuates proinflammatory cytokines and immune cells in healthy subjects. Nutrition Research. 2012;**32**(12):947-955. DOI: 10.1016/J.NUTRES.2012.06.021

[18] de Groot S et al. The effects of short-term fasting on tolerance to (neo) adjuvant chemotherapy in HER2-negative breast cancer patients: A randomized pilot study. BMC Cancer. 2015;**15**(1):476. DOI: 10.1186/s12885-018-4353-2

[19] Brandhorst S, Longo VD. Fasting and caloric restriction in cancer prevention and treatment. Recent Results in Cancer Research. 2016;**207**:241-266. DOI: 10.1007/978-3-319-42118-6_12

[20] Liberti MV, Locasale JW. The Warburg effect: How does it benefit cancer cells? Trends in Biochemical Sciences. 2016;**41**(3):287

[21] Bianchi G et al. Fasting induces anti-Warburg effect that increases respiration but reduces ATP-synthesis to promote apoptosis in colon cancer models. Oncotarget. 2015;**6**(14):11806-11819. DOI: 10.18632/ONCOTARGET.3688

[22] Vasconcelos AR et al. Intermittent fasting attenuates lipopolysaccharide-induced neuroinflammation and memory impairment. Journal of Neuroinflammation. 2014;**11**:85. DOI: 10.1186/1742-2094-11-85

[23] Hartman ML et al. Augmented growth hormone (GH) secretory burst frequency and amplitude mediate enhanced GH secretion during a two-day fast in normal men. The Journal of Clinical Endocrinology and Metabolism. 1992;**74**(4):757-765. DOI: 10.1210/JCEM.74.4.1548337

[24] Rui L. Energy metabolism in the liver. Comprehensive Physiology. 2014;**4**(1):177. DOI: 10.1002/CPHY.C130024

[25] Angoorani P, Ejtahed HS, Hasani-Ranjbar S, Siadat SD, Soroush AR, Larijani B. Gut microbiota modulation as a possible mediating mechanism for fasting-induced alleviation of metabolic complications: A systematic review. Nutrition and Metabolism (London). 2021;**18**(1):3. DOI: 10.1186/S12986-021-00635-3

[26] Doghri T, Beltaifa L, Bouguerra R, Ben Slama C, Jabrane H, El-Khadhi A, et al. Food intake, and anthropometrical and biological parameters in adult Tunisians during fasting at Ramadan. East Mediterranean Health Journal. 2002;**8**:603-611

[27] Gharbi M, Akrout M, Zouari B. Food intake during and outside Ramadan. East Mediterranean Health Journal. 2003;**9**:131-140

[28] Gjuladin-Hellon T, Davies IG, Penson P, Baghbadorani RA. Effects

of carbohydrate-restricted diets on low-density lipoprotein cholesterol levels in overweight and obese adults: A systematic review and meta-analysis. Nutrition Reviews. 2019;**77**(3):161-180. DOI: 10.1093/NUTRIT/NUY049

[29] Kerndt PR, Naughton JL, Driscoll CE, Loxterkamp DA. Fasting: The history, pathophysiology and complications. The Western Journal of Medicine. 1982;**137**(5):379-399

[30] Hoddy KK, Kroeger CM, Trepanowski JF, Barnosky AR, Bhutani S, Varady KA. Safety of alternate day fasting and effect on disordered eating behaviors. Nutrition Journal. 2015;**14**(1):1-3. DOI: 10.1186/S12937-015-0029-9/TABLES/2

[31] Harris L et al. Intermittent fasting interventions for the treatment of overweight and obesity in adults aged 18 years and over: A systematic review and meta-analysis executive summary background. JBI Database of Systematic Reviews and Implementation Reports;**16**(2):507-547. DOI: 10.11124/JBISRIR-2016

[32] Kumar S, Kaur G. Intermittent fasting dietary restriction regimen negatively influences reproduction in young rats: A study of hypothalamo-hypophysial-gonadal axis. PLoS One. 2013;**8**(1). DOI: 10.1371/JOURNAL.PONE.0052416

[33] Warner SO et al. Short-term fasting lowers glucagon levels under euglycemic and hypoglycemic conditions in healthy humans. JCI Insight. 2023;**8**(12). DOI: 10.1172/JCI.INSIGHT.169789

[34] Benau EM, Orloff NC, Janke EA, Serpell L, Timko CA. A systematic review of the effects of experimental fasting on cognition. Appetite. 2014;**77**:52-61. DOI: 10.1016/J.APPET.2014.02.014

[35] Crhová M, Kapounková K. Influence of long-term fasting and intermittent fasting on the cognitive abilities. Studia Sportiva. 2020;**14**(1):15-22. DOI: 10.5817/sts2020-1-2

[36] Mehanna HM, Moledina J, Travis J. Refeeding syndrome: What it is, and how to prevent and treat it. British Medical Journal. 2008;**336**(7659):1495. DOI: 10.1136/BMJ.A301

Chapter 3

Role of Fasting in Sport Exercise

Jonathan Fusi, Giorgia Scarfò and Ferdinando Franzoni

Abstract

Nowadays, the focus on health and nutrition has developed greatly. Literature data suggest that a healthy lifestyle is positively correlated with a reduction in numerous risk factors. In addition to the classic nutritional schemes, such as the Mediterranean diet or the Okinawa or vegan diet, fasting is becoming a choice that many people follow. But how many types of fasting are there? Are they all optimal? Are they advisable for all individuals? What is the impact of fasting on physical activity? Literature data show that glycaemic control, pre-workout meal and post-workout meal, are crucial for improved performance. But what are our body's adaptations to fasted training? As happens, for example, during the period of RAMADAN. Is there a sport in which fasting can be most useful for performance purposes?

Keywords: intermittent fasting, exercise, Ramadan, fasting, autophagy, sports nutrition

1. Introduction

This chapter aims to reassess the role of different intermittent fasting strategies in exercise nutrition.

Within the chapter, we will look at the concept of autophagy has been correlated with fasting and intermittent fasting. Furthermore, we will evaluate how this nutritional practice can primarily be useful in the improvement and treatment of numerous risk factors. Based on the scientific evidence, we will attempt to shed light on the numerous intermittent fasting methods applied to sport.

The aim of sports nutrition, especially in recent years, is to make the athlete perform. Performance is closely dependent on the intake of macronutrients, so much so that numerous strategies have been devised concerning the most correct type of supplementation or nutrient timing.

Nowadays, there are many different eating styles such as the Mediterranean diet, the vegetarian diet and the vegan diet. These nutritional patterns may change throughout the year, depending on body composition or types of training (off-season, in-season etc.) or religious beliefs such as Ramadan.

From a nutritional point of view, Ramadan is similar to intermittent fasting.

In recent years, the study of physical changes induced by intermittent fasting has undergone great development. In the following chapters, we will analyse the changes induced by fasting and intermittent fasting in athletes.

2. Why we came to study fasting and intermittent fasting?

Fasting is used as a practice to improve cellular function and reduce risk factors. Seems that this activity is related to improve cellular function such as autophagy [1]. Autophagy (eating by oneself) represents a process that facilitates the removal of misfolded or aggregated proteins and the eventual recycling of damaged cellular components [2, 3].

Three types of autophagy can be defined:

- Macroautophagy,
- Microautophagy
- Chaperone-mediated autophagy [4].

According to Glick et al. [4], autophagy plays a role in both protecting against genome instability and preventing necrosis [4]. From this evidence, it can be deduced that autophagy may play a role in the prevention of numerous diseases, including neurodegenerative diseases. In support of this, Rubinsztein in his work entitled "Autophagy and ageing" [5] notes how dysregulation of autophagy can be related to neurodegenerative disorders, metabolic diseases and even cancer.

The control mechanisms of autophagy are closely related to metabolic sensors such as mTOR and AMPK, which is why it was thought that nutrition could somehow have a direct effect [6].

These insights are due to the studies of Fabrizio and Longo [7]. In their study, the authors highlighted how calorie restriction is able to increase the Chronological Life Span (CLS) in yeasts [7]. This led to a series of subsequent studies confirming the findings [8, 9]. Not only that, it was subsequently observed that caloric restriction can lead to an increase in autophagy in cardiac and skeletal muscle and also in the liver [10, 11]. The promotion of autophagy thus appears to be a protective effect against cellular ageing.

According to scientific evidence, it therefore becomes clear that the method of calorie restriction understood as fasting and intermittent fasting should be investigated as useful methods in improving quality of life and reducing risk factors.

Intermittent fasting or fasting can, in fact, be seen as a specific reduction of daily calories, which in the long run can lead to metabolic adaptations that induce an increase in human lifespan [12].

From a literature review, we can see that the concept of intermittent fasting is represented by three major macro-areas:

- Time-restricted eating (TRE). Fasting period is most commonly >12 hours. Belonging to this category is the Ramadan fast (RDIF). This represents the fasting period during Ramadan, practised by Muslims from sunrise to sunset on consecutive days for a total duration of 1 month. In this particular type of nutritional scheme, energy restriction is not required.
- Alternate day fasting (ADF). Decrease of daily calorie intake to 25% for one day, followed by ad libitum feeding the next day, on a repeated basis. Or, we can observe a 24-hour fasting period for 1 day, followed by ad libitum feeding the next day. This pattern is also known as periodic fasting.

- Intermittent energy restriction (IER) or Intermittent Calorie Restriction (ICR). Less defined fasting period. The subject follows periods of energy restriction alternating with periods of habitual intake or minimally restricted diet [13, 14]. There are two forms: 2:5 (caloric restriction for 2 days a week, and a regular diet for 5 days) or 3:4 (caloric restriction for 3 days a week, and a regular diet for 4 days) [15].

In addition to these macro-areas, other declensions of fasting or intermittent fasting related to religion can be found. For example, members of the Church of Jesus Christ of Latter-day Saints habitually abstain from food and drink for long periods of time. Or, Seventh-day Adventists consume the last of their two daily meals in the afternoon, resulting in prolonged overnight fast [14].

Those listed above are macro-areas of differentiation of fasting. In fact, Laza [16] reports a more extensive classification and differentiation.

- 12:12 model – 12 h fasting and 12 h normal food intake

- 16:8 model – 8 hours represent the "food window" and 16 hours represent the "fasting window." It is a very flexible pattern. During the food window, there is no calorie control of food. The only caution is to take a constant amount of fluid to avoid dehydration.

- 20:4 model – 2 h fasting and 4 h food window (warrior diet)

- Full-day fasting (FDF) – 24 h fasting, to be repeated 2 to 3 times a week (Eat-Stop-Eat).

- In this scheme, the meal is rather low in calories and therefore the weekly calorie intake decreases.

- As described by Horne et al. [17], this type of diet is contraindicated for athletes practising endurance sports.

- 24-hour weekly fasting—This is complete fasting during 24 hours per week, in which only liquids are consumed; it is also referred to as water fasting [18, 19].

- 5:2 model – This is the most popular and most studied protocol. Characterised by 5 days of regular feeding and two days of fasting (which do not have to be consecutive).

- 36 h model – 36 h is the fasting window.

- Extended fasting model – 7 to 14 days. This model has very high vitamin, mineral and liquid risks [20].

The role and use of Fasting or Intermittent Fasting, not only for religious or purely research purposes, have undergone a breakthrough thanks to the book published by Mosley & Spencer in 2013 [21] entitled "*Fast-Diet*". In their book, the authors showed the benefits of severe calorie restriction (fasting-like) for 2 days, followed by a normal calorie intake for the rest of the week. Nutritional pattern is very similar to TRE [13]. This upsurge in research around intermittent fasting or fasting, has prompted many researchers to reveal the potential of this special type of nutritional scheme in relation to human health, such as the circadian rhythm, the gut microbiota/microbiome and modifiable lifestyles to both reduce risk factor prevention and in the treatment of chronic diseases [14].

3. Role of fasting and intermittent fasting in the prevention and treatment of numerous diseases

As we have seen in the previous chapter, there are at least three distinctions of intermittent fasting (TRE, ADF, IER), each of which is capable of inducing changes in the metabolic sphere, leading to potential positive effects on human health. Clearly, the first objective when using these methods is to keep weight under control or to reduce it. Obviously, associated with a decrease in weight is also a decrease in various related risk factors [22].

The change in visceral adipose tissue is a real parameter to be monitored [23] to assess cardiometabolic risk reduction [23].

In the study published by Trepanowski et al. [24], a 0.4 kg reduction in visceral fat mass was found after 6 and 12 months of Alternative-day Modified Fasting (AMDF), compared to a control group not subjected to dietary restriction. On the other hand, the reduction was superimposed on a calorie-restricted group, thus emphasising that perhaps it is only due to the calorie restriction and not the specific scheme.

Holmer et al. [25], took up the studies of Trepanowski [25]. In this study, the researchers showed that both weekly fasting and reduction of daily carbohydrates play a key role in reducing hepatic steatosis.

In a different way, all intervention schemes based on intermittent fasting or simply on calorie restriction would seem to be able to induce an improvement in cardiovascular risk factors. Alternate Day Fasting (ADF) would appear to reduce total cholesterol, triglyceride and LDL concentration and blood pressure, but not HDL cholesterol and blood glucose. In contrast, Time-Restricted Eating (TRE) has a powerful positive effect on reducing blood pressure and triglycerides, whereas it has no effect on LDL and HDL concentration [26–28]. In addition, intermittent fasting would appear to have a direct role in connection with numerous pathologies, both metabolic and central nervous system-related [29]. In this case, data from the literature are scarce, and, in some cases, it is interesting to note that the various meta-analyses also include the ketogenic diet due to the fasting characteristic [30]. The study published by Ooi et al. [31] is very interesting [31]. In his study, he evaluated the effect of intermittent fasting in subjects with mild cognitive impairment. The results showed that subjects practising intermittent fasting had better cognitive impairment scores than a control group. The study by Mindikoglu et al. [32] also obtained similar results. In this study, 14 healthy subjects were enrolled who were fasted from dawn to dusk (like Ramadan) for a total duration of 30 consecutive days. The data obtained from plasma evaluations showed an increase in anti-cancer proteins, improved insulin signalling, circadian rhythm and DNA repair mechanisms. In addition, they found improvements in biomarkers associated with cognitive function. The data obtained thus highlighted both a possible anticarcinogenic capacity and an improvement in cognitive function of intermittent fasting.

Animal models are also giving hope in the treatment or prevention of Parkinison's disease in relation to Fasting Mimicking Diet (FMD) or Time-Restricted Feeding (TRF) protocols [33, 34]. Unfortunately, there are yet no trials in humans, but data from mouse models bodes well [30]. From the literature data, however, it appears that the target is at the level of dopaminergic neurons and the gut microbiota.

Reviewing the literature data from the various studies on the interactions of the various types of fasting, the intestinal microbiota is one of the main targets. This fact should not come as a surprise as the intestinal bacterial flora is greatly affected by the type of nutritional pattern [35]. Literature studies affirm that TRF can bring about positive effects on the intestinal bacterial flora. In fact, an increase in short-chain fatty acids (SCFA), which act both as a substrate for the bacterial flora and as satiety signalling, is observed in connection with periods of TRF. This is achieved by activation of two receptors located on the surface of the intestinal wall called GRP41 and GRP43. Activation of GRP41 results in the production of peptide YY by enteroendocrine cells. Peptide YY is responsible for reducing the body's ability to absorb energy from food, also leading to changes in glucose utilisation [36, 37]. TRF appears to be able to bring about a modulation of the type of microorganisms present in the intestinal flora in addition to the production of SCFAs [38].

The study by Zeb et al. [39] in this respect is of great value. In fact, his study shows that the microorganism Prevotlla_9, Faecalibacterium, and Dialister were more abundant in the group subjected to TRF. Thus highlighting the fundamental role of TRF in modulating the population of microorganisms.

Also, with a view to investigating the changes induced by different types of fasting, Mousavi et al. [40] compare the Ramadan method and non-Ramadan fasting.

As is now well known, Ramadan is one of the most common types of fasting in which millions of Muslims around the world do not receive food or drink for a daily time varying between 12 and 22 hours (average 12–14 hours). The period may vary depending on geographical location and seasonality [41]. Fasting is not expected for children, pregnant and lactating women [40]. Since fasting is therefore a fast, various authors have tried to understand the possible effects on the microbiota induced by this type of diet. Mohammadzadeh et al. [42] showed that the serum level of butyrate (SCFA) was increased in subjects practising Ramadan for 1 month. An increase in Bacteroides and Filminus strains was also found in this parameter.

These data were also found in the study conducted by Su et al. [43]. In this study, it was shown that Ramadan improves the diversity of the microbiota with an upregulation of the butyric acid-producing Lachnospiraceae.

These changes in the gut microbiota could be an explanation for why different types of fasting would also appear to have an impact on sports performance.

4. Fasting and intermittent fasting on sports nutrition

Intermittent fasting or fasting can bring about positive metabolic adaptations and reduce various risk factors. This is why researchers have studied the possible relationships between these types of nutrition and metabolic response under stress [15]. The purpose of nutrition in sport is to maximise the training phase, leading to optimum post-training recovery and the right fuel during training. It is therefore essential that there is an optimal balance of macronutrients such as carbohydrates, fats and proteins without neglecting electrolyte balance.

The study of the effect of fasting on performance in elite athletes began around 2007, based on the beliefs of many athletes and coaches, who believed that fasting could have a negative impact on sports performance [44–46]. Among the various types of fasting, the Ramadan fast is gaining increasing importance. Indeed, being a fast of a religious nature, it can often occur during sporting competitions such as, for example, the London 2012 Olympic Games, the 2014 and 2022 FIFA World Cup [44, 47, 48].

Hence, as we will see later, it deserves its own section.

Before going on to evaluate the possible effects on performance induced by fasting or intermittent fasting, we must highlight the metabolic responses in acute and chronic.

When fasting is performed during activity, changes in both glycaemic and lipid response are observed in the acute phase [15].

In acute we observe changes in the glycaemic curve. In fact, there is an elevated glucose concentration up to 6 h after the meal, then decreasing over the remaining 16 h. During the remaining 16 h, there is a decrease in insulin activity in favour of an increase in glucagon (to stimulate lipolysis) and sympathetic activity [49]. In association with this response, as one might expect, there is an increase in free fatty acids (FFA) and ketone bodies, with a final stimulation of gluconeogenesis 6. During fasting FFA and ketone bodies become the main source of cellular energy that goes by the name of glucose-ketone (G-to-K) switchover.

In this specific scenario, an important role is also observed in the energy provided by protein metabolism, where normally its relevance is much less [50, 51]. In contrast, there are many studies in the literature concerning the adaptations of various types of fasting in chronic [51–54].

In chronic conditions, changes in body composition and metabolic response are observed [15].

The literature confirms that this type of diet is able to bring about both a reduction in weight [54, 55] and an improvement in body composition, with a decrease in fat mass [54–56]. If, however, we carefully analyse the data, as carried out in a review by Zouhal et al. [15], we can see that in general, all low-calorie diets, especially the various types of fasting lead to a loss of weight and fat mass. On the other hand, however, it is worth emphasising how difficult the studies are to analyse as it is not always easy to control the participants and there are many variables to be considered [15].

Chronic metabolic responses seem to correlate with what happens in terms of body composition. In fact, there are alterations in lipid and glucose metabolism. Hammouda et al. [57] found that fasting can lead to a decrease in serum low-density lipoprotein-cholesterol (LDL-C), total cholesterol (TC), triglycerides (TG). In contrast, fasting protocols appear to result in an increase in high-density lipoprotein-cholesterol (HDL-C) levels.

Applying this type of diet to physical activity, the results reported in the literature are manifold but sometimes contradictory to each other due to the heterogeneity of treatment and population studied [58–61].

To understand the possible adaptations in terms of performance, induced by fasting and intermittent fasting, it is useful to divide the type of physical activity in relation to the substrates used. In fact, we are going to talk about aerobic activity, where oxygen is the determining factor that induces the oxidation of carbohydrates (aerobic glycolysis) and lipids (fatty acid bet-oxidation), with a moderate production of lactate [62]. By contrast, the term anaerobic activity is used to refer to the types of exercise in which carbohydrates are used as the primary source of energy (anaerobic glycolysis) with high lactate production [63].

What seems to be certain is the ability of intermittent fasting to reduce the percentage of fat mass independently of the type of exercise practised. In support of this, it is useful to report some rather interesting studies.

Martínez-Rodríguez et al. [64] divided two groups of 14 women. One group underwent a period of intermittent fasting combined with a high-intensity interval training (HIIT) protocol. The other group was treated with HIIT. The data obtained showed a decrease in the percentage of fat mass in the first group. Hosseini et al. [65] also showed that in a group of 50 healthy subjects, the use of intermittent fasting-induced a decrease in the percentage of fat mass and an improvement in the body mass index (BMI).

Dorand et al. [66] highlighted the role of intermittent fasting (IF) and a possible association with aerobic exercise performance in 40 Wistar rats, divided into four groups: sedentary, trained, intermittent fasting and intermittent fasting with training. In this case, aerobic training was used (30 min, five times per week at a speed of 15 m/min) for a total duration of 4 weeks. Subjected to intermittent fasting. The data obtained showed that in the group trained and subjected to intermittent fasting, there was a loss of muscle mass and muscle damage, but performance was not impaired [66]. The loss of muscle mass appears to be a phenomenon that occurs precisely induced by fasting, as shown in another study also on rats [67]. In fact, the pre-workout meal, but especially the post-workout meal, characterised by an optimal ratio of carbohydrates to protein is fundamental for improving body composition and maximising training [68]. Interesting, however, is the non-decrease in performance, so it would seem that an adaptive mechanism is present in rats. It is worth mentioning that loss of lean mass has not always been found, probably when IF is associated with exercise, the latter may be able to mitigate the loss of lean mass [69, 70]. The result obtained by Dorand et al. [66] regarding the interaction between IF and no decrease in performance was also observed previously by Tovar et al. [71]. In this study, the authors examined the effects of time restricting feeding (TRF) 16/8 on endurance performance in male runners. The duration of the study was four weeks. At the end of the experimental period, the authors found a decrease in fat mass. In performance terms, the researchers found an improvement in blood lactate concentration, thus underlining a better ability in the use of energy substrates in the unit of time. This parameter is significant in performance terms. Not only that, but the researchers also concluded that they did not find a decrease in lean mass [71]. The problem with the fasting state during training is to try to understand how the metabolism manages to cope with energy demand during both endurance and interval or resistance training.

In this regard, the review published by Vicente-Salar et al. [72] attempts to evaluate the studies in the literature concerning the metabolic adaptations observed in various endurance training and fasting sate protocols. The aim of the study was to evaluate whether training under fasting conditions could promote the utilisation of fatty acids. This shift would counteract low glycogen levels, thus leading to both performance improvement and weight control. Clearly, this concept can only apply in this case, as during endurance training the substrate most frequently utilised are fatty acids [62]. Literature data showed that fasting during endurance training around 25–44% of VO_2max or around 70%VO2max would appear to increase blood levels of glycerol and fatty acids [72]. It should be noted that there would appear to be a shift between substrates to ensure continued exercise. It can be seen, however, that VO_2max percentages appear to be decisive, in fact, representing a work intensity it is easy to understand how at values above 80% there would appear to be no such shift precisely because of the difficulty that beta oxidation may have in supplying energy in the unit of time [73].

In terms of performance, the data are conflicting. Naharudin et al. [59] investigated the role of the interaction between intermittent fasting and high-intensity exercise in a group of 20 subjects for a total duration of 10 days. The parameters investigated were the Wingate test, body and aerobic exercise. The results showed a decrease in the parameters in the first few moments, which is explained by the researchers as requiring a timing of more than 10 days to have a sensitive metabolic adaptation to fasting. To bring some order to the many studies relating the effects of intermittent fasting on performance, the meta-analysis by Correia et al. [74] is very interesting. This article reports on the most interesting studies in which an attempt is made to relate the various types of fasting and the various adaptive responses in terms of performance.

In his paper, Correia notes that many studies find that the use of intermittent fasting can lead to improvements in either strength (increased jump) or aerobic capacity (in terms of VO2max and decreased VCO2). However, as we can imagine, the data are in contrast to each other, for in the study conducted by Moro et al. [75] in which 16 young cyclists were subjected to intermittent fasting (16/8) for a duration of 4 weeks, changes in metabolism and body composition were observed, but no alteration in performance. Also, in the study by Tovar et al. [71], no performance changes were reported in a group of 15 male runners subjected to intermittent fasting (16/8), where improvements in terms of body composition, stress test and 10 km test were observed.

4.1 Ramadan and physical exercise

Ramadan represents the eighth pillar of Islam and is classified as a specific form of intermittent fasting, as it refers to a specific time of year in accordance with the Muslim calendar. During this period, Muslim adults in good health undergo a period of intermittent fasting for 29–30 consecutive days. Muslims abstain from eating and drinking from sunrise to sunset, refraining only at night [76]. In contrast to other types of fasting, in the latter, subjects do not even have to drink or chew [77]. As evidenced by several studies, food intake during the night determines significant changes in athletes in terms of meal composition, hydration status, and sleep quality and quantity [77–79]. All these variables could induce alterations in terms of sports performance. In fact, many Muslim athletes report a greater feeling of fatigue, especially in high-intensity exercises. However, it should be emphasised that these feelings are subjective [80, 81]. Triki et al. [82] sought to understand whether Ramadan could interfere with the adaptations induced by a resistance training (RT) protocol by subjecting 20 subjects practising whole-body RT in the late afternoon on a fasted state (FAST) and 20 training in the late evening in a fed state (FED). The results show that FAST did not lead to any negative effects in terms of hypertrophy and strength. On the other hand, the best results were obtained during the FED state. Far more interesting are probably the studies investigating the possible effect of Ramadan on endurance sports. In endurance sports, there is both an important utilisation of carbohydrates and fatty acids and an increase in sweating. The increase of sweating is the reason why training in a state of both food and fluid fasting can affect performance. Khemila et al. [83] investigated the possible effects of Ramadan on cognitive and physical performance in football players. The players were subjected to assessment tests such as the 30-second Wingate test, and cognitive tests such as the mental rotation test (MRT) and selective attention test (SA) and the Pittsburgh Sleep Quality Index (PSQI) during the four weeks of Ramadan. The results showed that anaerobic performance was not affected in the morning but in the evening. Obviously, this was due to the glycogen load during the evening feeding phase. The results on sleep quality were interesting; in fact, they were found to have improved during the last two weeks of Ramadan. To summarise, even on the basis of a well-structured review [84], it can be observed that the literature data are contradictory. Indeed, negative effects on performance are found to be due to rest and hydration. it appears that negative effects on performance appear during Ramadan (14/10), which may be due to other aspects such as rest and hydration. The negative effects have been found to be most pronounced in elite athletes.

5. Conclusion

Intermittent fasting represents a new frontier in nutrition applied to sport. Nutrition in the sense of calculating macronutrients and timing, is an essential ally for the sportsman. Researchers began to study it around 2007, until it reached peak interest, especially for Ramadan, during the London 2012 Olympic Games and also the 2014 and 2022 FIFA World Cup as these events took place during the month of Ramadan [44, 48]. The term intermittent fasting refers to a nutritional practice in which the subject eats within a certain window and fasts the rest of the time. In clinical terms, intermittent fasting appears to have excellent results in weight control and body recomposition, as well as having a potential preventive effect on chronic diseases.

Although there are many types of intermittent fasting, competing or training in endurance sports during fasting could be counterproductive. In contrast, strength or anaerobic sports, especially during Ramadan, if done in the morning, do not seem to be affected. We must not generalise; it takes a long time to adapt to this nutritional pattern and often not everyone is able to follow it. In fact, many athletes need a pre-training meal to maximise results [84].

When Ramadan is followed, on the other hand, the nutritional practice needs to be well versed in the pros and cons of this dietary pattern in order to be able to help the athlete throughout the fasting period while maximising results and preventing problems such as dehydration. In conclusion, further research is needed to explore the interaction between IF and exercise performance. All variables must be carefully monitored and evaluated to understand adaptations and it is critical to understand the parallel energy and metabolic pathways that are activated during fasting.

Acknowledgements

Jonathan Fusi has conceived and written the work, has found the bibliography of reference. Giorgia Scarfò has rechecked the bibliography and the grammar, Ferdinando Franzoni has supervised the manuscript.

Conflict of interest

The authors declare no conflit of interest.

Author details

Jonathan Fusi, Giorgia Scarfò and Ferdinando Franzoni*
Department of Clinical and Experimental Medicine, University of PISA, Pisa, Italy

*Address all correspondence to: ferdinando.franzoni@unipi.it

References

[1] Bagherniya M, Butler AE, Barreto GE, Sahebkar A. The effect of fasting or calorie restriction on autophagy induction: A review of the literature. Ageing Research Reviews. 2018;**47**:183-197. DOI: 10.1016/j.arr.2018.08.004

[2] Xie Z, Klionsky DJ. Autophagosome formation: Core machinery and adaptations. Nature Cell Biology. 2007;**9**(10):1102-1109. DOI: 10.1038/ncb1007-1102

[3] Choi AMK, Ryter SW, Levine B. Autophagy in human health and disease. The New England Journal of Medicine. 2013;**368**:651-662

[4] Glick D, Barth S, Macleod KF. Autophagy: Cellular and molecular mechanisms. The Journal of Pathology. 2010;**221**(1):3-12

[5] Rubinsztein DC, Codogno P, Levine B. Autophagy modulation as a potential therapeutic target for diverse diseases. Nature Reviews. Drug Discovery. 2012;**11**(9):709

[6] Liu S, Yao S, Yang H, Liu S, Wang Y. Autophagy: Regulator of cell death. Cell Death & Disease. 2023;**14**(10):648. DOI: 10.1038/s41419-023-06154-8

[7] Fabrizio P, Longo VD. The chronological life span of Saccharomyces cerevisiae. Aging Cell. 2003;**2**(2):73-81. DOI: 10.1046/j.1474-9728.2003.00033.x

[8] Jia K, Levine B. Autophagy is required for dietary restriction-mediated life span extension in C. Elegans. Autophagy. 2007;**3**:597-599. DOI: 10.4161/auto.4989

[9] Mörck C, Pilon M. *C. Elegans* feeding defective mutants have shorter body lengths and increased autophagy. BMC Developmental Biology. 2006;**6**:39. DOI: 10.1186/1471-213X-6-39

[10] Wohlgemuth SE, Julian D, Akin DE, Fried J, Toscano K, Leeuwenburgh C, et al. Autophagy in the heart and liver during normal aging and calorie restriction. Rejuvenation Research. 2007;**10**:281-292. DOI: 10.1089/REJ.2006.0535

[11] Donati A, Cavallini G, Bergamini E. Effects of aging, antiaging calorie restriction and in vivo stimulation of autophagy on the urinary excretion of 8OHdG in male Sprague-Dawley rats. Age (Dordrecht, Netherlands). 2013;**35**(2):261-270. DOI: 10.1007/s11357-011-9346-x

[12] Madeo F, Carmona-Gutierrez D, Hofer SJ, Kroemer G. Caloric restriction Mimetics against age-associated disease: Targets, mechanisms, and therapeutic potential. Cell Metabolism. 2019;**29**(3):592-610. DOI: 10.1016/j.cmet.2019.01.018

[13] Lange MG, Coffey AA, Coleman PC, Barber TM, Van Rens T, Oyebode O, et al. Metabolic changes with intermittent fasting. Journal of Human Nutrition and Dietetics. 2024;**37**(1):256-269. DOI: 10.1111/jhn.13253

[14] Patterson RE, Sears DD. Metabolic effects of intermittent fasting. Annual Review of Nutrition. 2017;**21**(37):371-393. DOI: 10.1146/annurev-nutr-071816-064634

[15] Zouhal H, Saeidi A, Salhi A, Li H, Essop MF, Laher I, et al. Exercise training and fasting: Current insights. Open access Journal of Sports Medicine. 2020;**21**(11):1-28. DOI: 10.2147/OAJSM.S224919

[16] Laza V. Intermittent fasting in athletes: PROs and CONs. Health, Sports & Rehabilitation Medicine. 2020;**21**(1):52-58

[17] Horne BD, Muhlestein JB, Lappe DL, May HT, Carlquist JF, Galenko O, et al. Randomized cross-over trial of short-term water-only fasting: Metabolic and cardiovascular consequences. Nutrition, Metabolism, and Cardiovascular Diseases. 2013;**23**(11):1050-1057. DOI: 10.1016/j.numecd.2012.09.007

[18] Nowosad K, Sujka M. Effect of various types of intermittent fasting (IF) on weight loss and improvement of diabetic parameters in human. Current Nutrition Reports. Jun 2021;**10**(2):146-154. DOI: 10.1007/s13668-021-00353-5. Epub 2021 Apr 7

[19] Patikorn C, Roubal K, Veettil SK, Chandran V, Pham T, Lee YY, et al. Intermittent fasting and obesity-related health outcomes: An umbrella review of meta-analyses of randomized clinical trials. JAMA Netw Open. 1 Dec 2021;**4**(12):e2139558. DOI: 10.1001/jamanetworkopen.2021.39558

[20] Bertile F, Fouillen L, Wasselin T, Pauline M, Yvon LM, Van Dorsselaer A, et al. The safety limits of an extended fast: Lessons from a non-model organism. Scientific Reports. 2016;**6**:39008. DOI: 10.1038/srep39008

[21] Mosley M, Spencer M. The FastDiet: Lose Weight, Stay Healthy, and Live longer with the Simple Secret of Intermittent Fasting. New York: Atria; 2013

[22] Pagidipati NJ, Nelson AJ, Kaltenbach LA, Leyva M, McGuire DK, Pop-Busui R, et al. Coordinated care to optimize cardiovascular preventive therapies in type 2 diabetes: A randomized clinical trial. Journal of the American Medical Association. 2023;**329**(15):1261-1270. DOI: 10.1001/jama.2023.2854

[23] Dote-Montero M, Sanchez-Delgado G, Ravussin E. Effects of intermittent fasting on Cardiometabolic health: An energy metabolism perspective. Nutrients. 2022;**14**(3):489. DOI: 10.3390/nu14030489

[24] Trepanowski JF, Kroeger CM, Barnosky A, Klempel MC, Bhutani S, Hoddy KK, et al. Effect of alternate-day fasting on weight loss, weight maintenance, and Cardioprotection among metabolically healthy obese adults: A randomized clinical trial. JAMA Internal Medicine. 2017;**177**:930-938. DOI: 10.1001/jamainternmed.2017.0936

[25] Holmer M, Lindqvist C, Petersson S, Moshtaghi-Svensson J, Tillander V, Brismar TB, et al. Treatment of NAFLD with intermittent calorie restriction or low-carb high-fat diet—A randomised controlled trial. JHEP Reports. 2021;**3**(3):100256. DOI: 10.1016/j.jhepr.2021.100256

[26] Cui Y, Cai T, Zhou Z, Mu Y, Lu Y, Gao Z, et al. Health effects of alternate-day fasting in adults: A systematic review and meta-analysis. Frontiers in Nutrition. 2020;7:586036. DOI: 10.3389/fnut.2020.586036

[27] Moon S, Kang J, Kim SH, Chung HS, Kim YJ, Yu JM, et al. Beneficial effects of time-restricted eating on metabolic diseases: A systemic review and meta-analysis. Nutrients. 2020;**12**:1267

[28] Pureza I, Macena ML, da Silva Junior AE, Praxedes DRS, Vasconcelos LGL, Bueno NB. Effect of early time-restricted feeding on the metabolic profile of adults with excess weight: A systematic review with meta-analysis. Clinical Nutrition. 2021;**40**:1788-1799. DOI: 10.1016/j.clnu.2020.10.031

[29] Mattson MP, Longo VD, Harvie M. Impact of intermittent fasting on health and disease processes. Ageing Research Reviews. 2017;**39**:46-58. DOI: 10.1016/j.arr.2016.10.005

[30] Gudden J, Arias Vasquez A, Bloemendaal M. The effects of intermittent fasting on brain and cognitive function. Nutrients. 2021;**13**:3166. DOI: 10.3390/nu13093166

[31] Ooi TC, Meramat A, Rajab NF, Shahar S, Ismail IS, Azam AA, et al. Intermittent fasting enhanced the cognitive function in older adults with mild cognitive impairment by inducing biochemical and metabolic changes: A 3-year progressive study. Nutrients. 2020;**12**:2644. DOI: 10.3390/nu12092644

[32] Mindikoglu AL, Abdulsada MM, Jain A, Choi JM, Jalal PK, Devaraj S, et al. Intermittent fasting from dawn to sunset for 30 consecutive days is associated with anticancer proteomic signature and upregulates key regulatory proteins of glucose and lipid metabolism, circadian clock, DNA repair, cytoskeleton remodeling, immune system. Journal of Proteomics. 2020;**217**:103645. DOI: 10.1016/j.jprot.2020.103645

[33] Zhou ZL, Jia XB, Sun MF, Zhu YL, Qiao CM, Zhang BP, et al. Neuroprotection of fasting mimicking diet on MPTP-induced Parkinson's disease mice via gut microbiota and metabolites. Neurotherapeutics. 2019;**16**:741-760. DOI: 10.1007/s13311-019-00719-2

[34] Maswood N, Young J, Tilmont E, Zhang Z, Gash DM, Gerhardt GA, et al. Caloric restriction increases neurotrophic factor levels and attenuates neurochemical and behavioral deficits in a primate model of Parkinson's disease. Proceedings of the National Academy of Sciences of the United States of America. 2004;**101**:18171-18176. DOI: 10.1073/pnas.0405831102

[35] Beam A, Clinger E, Hao L. Effect of diet and dietary components on the composition of the gut microbiota. Nutrients. 2021;**13**(8):2795. DOI: 10.3390/nu13082795

[36] Sonnenburg JL, Bäckhed F. Diet-microbiota interactions as moderators of human metabolism. Nature. 2016;**535**(7610):56-64. DOI: 10.1038/nature18846

[37] Kobyliak N, Virchenko O, Falalyeyeva T. Pathophysiological role of host microbiota in the development of obesity. Nutrition Journal. 2016;**23**(15):43. DOI: 10.1186/s12937-016-0166-9

[38] Popa AD, Niță O, Gherasim A, Enache AI, Caba L, Mihalache L, et al. A scoping review of the relationship between intermittent fasting and the human gut microbiota: Current knowledge and future directions. Nutrients. 2023;**15**(9):2095. DOI: 10.3390/nu15092095

[39] Zeb F, Wu X, Chen L, Fatima S, Ijaz-Ul-Haq, Chen A, et al. Time-restricted feeding is associated with changes in human gut micro-biota related to nutrient intake. Nutrition. Oct 2020;**78**:110797. DOI: 10.1016/j.nut.2020.110797

[40] Mousavi SN, Rayyani E, Heshmati J, Tavasolian R, Rahimlou M. Effects of Ramadan and non-ramadan intermittent fasting on gut microbiome. Frontiers in Nutrition. 2022;**9**:860575. DOI: 10.3389/fnut.2022.860575

[41] Rashed AH. The fast of Ramadan. BMJ. 1992;**304**:521-522. DOI: 10.1136/bmj.304.6826.521

[42] Mohammadzadeh A, Roshanravan N, Mesri Alamdari N, Safaiyan A,

Mosharkesh E, Hadi A, et al. The interplay between fasting, gut microbiota, and lipid profile. International Journal of Clinical Practice. 2021;**75**:e14591. DOI: 10.1111/ijcp.14591

[43] Su J, Wang Y, Zhang X, Ma M, Xie Z, Pan Q, et al. Remodeling of the gut microbiome during Ramadan–associated intermittent fasting. The American Journal of Clinical Nutrition. 2021;**113**:1332-1342. DOI: 10.1093/ajcn/nqaa388

[44] Chaouachi A, Coutts AJ, Chamari K, Wong del P, Chaouachi M, Chtara M, et al. Effect of Ramadan intermittent fasting on aerobic and anaerobic performance and perception of fatigue in male elite judo athletes. Journal of Strength and Conditioning Research. 2009;**23**(9):2702-2709. DOI: 10.1519/JSC.0b013e3181bc17fc

[45] Karli U, Guvenc A, Aslan A, Hazir T, Acikada C. Influence of Ramadan fasting on anaerobic performance and recovery following short time high intensity exercise. Journal of Sports Science and Medicine. 2007;**6**(4):490

[46] Kirkendall DT, Leiper JB, Bartagi Z, Dvorak J, Zerguini Y. The influence of Ramadan on physical performance measures in young Muslim footballers. Journal of Sports Sciences. 2008;**26**(S3):S15-S27. DOI: 10.1080/02640410802422199

[47] Maughan R, Fallah J, Coyle EF. The effects of fasting on metabolism and performance. British Journal of Sports Medicine. 2010;**44**(7):490-494. DOI: 10.1136/bjsm.2010.07218

[48] Aloui A, Chtourou H, Hammouda O, Souissi H, Chaouachi A, Chamari K, et al. Effects of Ramadan on the diurnal variations of physical performance and perceived exertion in adolescent soccer players. Biological Rhythm Research. 2013;**44**(6):869-875. DOI: 10.1080/09291016.2013.780697

[49] Azizi F. Islamic fasting and health. Annals of Nutrition & Metabolism. 2010;**56**(4):273-282. DOI: 10.1159/000295848

[50] Cherif A, Roelands B, Meeusen R, Chamari K. Effects of intermittent fasting, caloric restriction, and Ramadan intermittent fasting on cognitive performance at rest and during exercise in adults. Sports Medicine. 2016;**46**(1):35-47. DOI: 10.1007/s40279-015-0408-6

[51] Solianik R, Sujeta A, Terentjevienė A, Skurvydas A. Effect of 48 h fasting on autonomic function, brain activity, cognition, and mood in amateur weight lifters. BioMed Research International. 2016;**2016**:1503956. DOI: 10.1155/2016/1503956

[52] Hussin N, Shahar S, Teng N, Ngah W, Das S. Efficacy of fasting and calorie restriction (FCR) on mood and depression among ageing men. The Journal of Nutrition, Health & Aging. 2013;**17**(8):674-680. DOI: 10.1007/s12603-013-0344-9

[53] Teng NIMF, Shahar S, Rajab NF, Manaf ZA, Johari MH, Ngah WZW. Improvement of metabolic parameters in healthy older adult men following a fasting calorie restriction intervention. The Aging Male. 2013;**16**(4):177-183. DOI: 10.3109/13685538.2013.832191

[54] Fitzgerald KC, Vizthum D, Henry-Barron B, Schweitzer A, Cassard SD, Kossoff E, et al. Effect of intermittent vs. daily calorie restriction on changes in weight and patient-reported outcomes in people with multiple sclerosis. Multiple Sclerosis and Related Disorders. 2018;**23**:33-39. DOI: 10.1016/j.msard.2018.05.002

[55] Klempel MC, Kroeger CM, Bhutani S, Trepanowski JF, Varady KA. Intermittent fasting combined with calorie restriction is effective for weight loss and cardio-protection in obese women. Nutrition Journal. 2012;**11**(1):98. DOI: 10.1186/1475-2891-11-98

[56] Teng NIMF, Shahar S, Manaf ZA, Das SK, Taha CSC, Ngah WZW. Efficacy of fasting calorie restriction on quality of life among aging men. Physiology & Behavior. 2011;**104**(5):1059-1064. DOI: 10.1016/j.physbeh.2011.07.007

[57] Hammouda O, Chtourou H, Aloui A, Arbi Mejri M, Chahed H, Miled A, et al. Does Ramadan fasting affect the diurnal variations in metabolic responses and total antioxidant capacity during exercise in young soccer players? Sport Sciences for Health. 2014;**10**(2):97-104. DOI: 10.1007/s11332-014-0179-8

[58] Aird TP, Davies RW, Carson BP. Effects of fasted vs fed-state exercise on performance and post-exercise metabolism: A systematic review and meta-analysis. Scandinavian Journal of Medicine & Science in Sports. 2018;**28**(5):1476-1493. DOI: 10.1111/sms.13054

[59] Bin, Naharudin MN, Yusof A. The effect of 10 days of intermittent fasting on Wingate anaerobic power and prolonged high-intensity time-to-exhaustion cycling performance. European Journal of Sport Science. 2018;**18**(5):667-676. DOI: 10.1080/17461391.2018.1438520

[60] Moro T, Tinsley G, Bianco A, Marcolin G, Pacelli QF, Battaglia G, et al. Effects of eight weeks of time-restricted feeding (16/8) on basal metabolism, maximal strength, body composition, inflammation, and cardiovascular risk factors in resistance-trained males. Journal of Translational Medicine. 2016;**14**(1):1-10. DOI: 10.1186/s12967-016-1044-0

[61] Tinsley GM, La Bounty PM. Effects of intermittent fasting on body composition and clinical health markers in humans. Nutrition Reviews. 2015;**73**(10):661-674. DOI: 10.1093/nutrit/nuv041

[62] Van Loon LJC, Greenhaff PL, Constantin-Teodosiu D, Saris WHM, Wagenmakers AJM. The effects of increasing exercise intensity on muscle fuel utilisation in humans. The Journal of Physiology. 2001;**536**:295-304. DOI: 10.1111/j.1469-7793.2001.00295.x

[63] Fusi J, Scarfò G, Franzoni F. Lactate: Anaerobic threshold and new discoveries. In: Wojda T editor. Technology in Sports—Recent Advances, New Perspectives and Application. 1st ed. 2023. IntechOpen; 2024. pp. 103-122. DOI: 10.5772/intechopen.1003067

[64] Martínez-Rodríguez A, Rubio-Arias JA, Frutos JMGD, Vicente-Martínez M, Gunnarsson TP. Effect of high-intensity interval training and intermittent fasting on body composition and physical performance in active women. International Journal of Environmental Research and Public Health. 2021;**18**:6431. DOI: 10.3390/ijerph18126431

[65] Hosseini S, Hejazi K. Evaluation of changes in blood hematological and biochemical parameters in response to Islamic fasting and regular physical activity in male and female subjects. Journal of Fasting and Health. 2015;**3**:118-125

[66] Dorand VAM, Soares NL, da Silva Andrade AA, Ribeiro MD, de Almeida Filho EJB, Neto MM, et al. Intermittent fasting associated with aerobic exercise improves oxidative parameters and causes muscle damage without

compromising the performance of Wistar rats. Nutrition. 2023;**115**:112159. DOI: 10.1016/j.nut.2023.112159

[67] das Neves W, de Oliveira LF, Da Silva RP, Alves CRR, Lancha AH. Fasting: A major limitation for resistance exercise training effects in rodents. Brazilian Journal of Medical and Biological Research. 2018;**51**:1-6. DOI: 10.1590/1414-431X20175427

[68] Jäger R, Kerksick CM, Campbell BI, Cribb PJ, Wells SD, Skwiat TM, et al. International Society of Sports Nutrition Position Stand: Protein and exercise. Journal of the International Society of Sports Nutrition. 2017;**20**(14):20. DOI: 10.1186/s12970-017-0177-8

[69] Ahmed I, Maughan RJ, Iqbal Z, Ali K, Naji O, Awan S, et al. Competing in the Ramadan fasted state: For spirituality, health and performance. British Journal of Sports Medicine. 2022;**56**:1001-1002

[70] Kang J, Ratamess NA, Faigenbaum AD, Bush JA, Beller N, Vargas A, et al. Effect of time restricted feeding on anthropometric, metabolic, and fitness parameters: A systematic review. Journal of the American Nutrition Association. 2022;**41**:810-825. DOI: 10.1080/07315724.2021.1958719

[71] Tovar AP, Richardson CE, Keim NL, Van Loan MD, Davis BA, Casazza GA. Four weeks of 16/8 time restrictive feeding in endurance trained male runners decreases fat mass, without affecting exercise performance. Nutrients. 2021;**13**:2941. DOI: 10.3390/nu13092941

[72] Vicente-Salar N, Urdampilleta Otegui A, Roche CE. Endurance training in fasting conditions: Biological adaptations and body weight management. Nutrición Hospitalaria. 2015;**32**(6):2409-2420. DOI: 10.3305/nh.2015.32.6.9488

[73] Houston ME. Biochemistry Primer for Exercise Science. 3rd ed. Human Kinetics Edition, Calzetti Mariucci (Italian Edition); 2008. pp. 45-77

[74] Correia JM, Santos I, Pezarat-Correia P, Minderico C, Mendonca GV. Effects of intermittent fasting on specific exercise performance outcomes: A systematic review including meta-analysis. Nutrients. 2020;**12**(5):1390. DOI: 10.3390/nu12051390

[75] Moro T, Tinsley G, Longo G, Grigoletto D, Bianco A, Ferraris C, et al. Time-restricted eating effects on performance, immune function, and body composition in elite cyclists: A randomized controlled trial. Journal of the International Society of Sports Nutrition. 2020;**17**:65. DOI: 10.1186/s12970-020-00396-z

[76] DeLang MD, Salamh PA, Chtourou H, Saad HB, Chamari K. The effects of Ramadan intermittent fasting on football players and implications for domestic football leagues over the next decade: A systematic review. Sports Medicine. 2022;**52**(3):585-600. DOI: 10.1007/s40279-021-01586-8

[77] Boukhris O, Hsouna H, Chtourou L, Abdesalem R, BenSalem S, Tahri N, et al. Effect of Ramadan fasting on feelings, dietary intake, rating of perceived exertion and repeated high intensity short-term maximal performance. Chronobiology International. 2019;**36**:1-10. DOI: 10.1080/07420528.2018.1513943

[78] Faris MEAIE, Jahrami HA, Alhayki FA, Alkhawaja NA, Ali AM, Aljeeb SH, et al. Effect of diurnal fasting on sleep during Ramadan: A systematic review and meta-analysis.

Sleep & Breathing. 2020;**24**:771-782. DOI: 10.1007/s11325-019-01986-1

[79] Romdhani M, Ammar A, Trabelsi K, Chtourou H, Vitale J, Masmoudi L, et al. Ramadan observance exacerbated the negative effects of COVID-19 lockdown on sleep and training behaviors: A international survey on 1,681 Muslim athletes. Frontiers in Nutrition. 2022;**9**:925092. DOI: 10.3389/fnut.2022.92509

[80] Trabelsi K, Stannard SR, Chtourou H, Moalla W, Ghozzi H, Jamoussi K, et al. Monitoring athletes' hydration status and sleep patterns during Ramadan observance: Methodological and practical considerations. Biological Rhythm Research. 2018;**49**:337-365. DOI: 10.1080/09291016.2017.1368214

[81] Hsouna H, Boukhris O, Trabelsi K, Abdessalem R, Ammar A, Irandoust K, et al. Effects of 25-min nap opportunity during Ramadan observance on the 5-m shuttle run performance and the perception of fatigue in physically active men. International Journal of Environmental Research and Public Health. 2020;**17**:3135. DOI: 10.3390/ijerph17093135

[82] Triki R, Zouhal H, Chtourou H, Salhi I, Jebabli N, Saeidi A, et al. Timing of resistance training during Ramadan fasting and its effects on muscle strength and hypertrophy. International Journal of Sports Physiology and Performance. 2023;**18**(6):579-589. DOI: 10.1123/ijspp.2022-0268

[83] Khemila S, Romdhani M, Farjallah MA, Abid R, Bentouati E, Souissi MA, et al. Effects of Ramadan fasting on the diurnal variations of physical and cognitive performances at rest and after exercise in professional football players. Frontiers in Psychology. 2023;**28**(14):1148845. DOI: 10.3389/fpsyg.2023.1148845

[84] Conde-Pipó J, Mora-Fernandez A, Martinez-Bebia M, Gimenez-Blasi N, Lopez-Moro A, Latorre JA, et al. Intermittent fasting: Does it affect sports performance? A systematic review. Nutrients. 2024;**16**:168. DOI: 10.3390/nu16010168

Chapter 4

Tapping into Immune Resilience: Exploring the Interplay between Fasting and Immune Function

Rakesh Kumar Jha and Ankita Kondhalkar

Abstract

Fasting, the voluntary abstention from food for specific periods, has been practiced for centuries, often tied to religious, spiritual, or cultural traditions. In recent decades, fasting has gained significant attention in the scientific community due to its potential health benefits, particularly regarding metabolic, cognitive, and immune functions. Various types of fasting, such as intermittent fasting, prolonged fasting, and time-restricted eating, have been explored for their impact on human physiology. The physiological changes triggered by fasting, including shifts in energy metabolism, activation of autophagy, and modulation of hormone levels, suggest a wide range of health implications. Fasting has been shown to improve insulin sensitivity, reduce inflammation, and enhance fat metabolism, making it an appealing strategy for weight management and disease prevention. Moreover, research indicates that fasting can promote cellular repair mechanisms and enhance immune resilience, which may contribute to longevity and the reduction of age-related diseases. Despite the growing interest, the long-term effects of fasting, particularly in diverse populations with varying health conditions, remain a topic of ongoing research. Understanding the mechanisms and outcomes of fasting is essential to determining its potential role in health promotion and disease prevention.

Keywords: fasting, metabolism, autophagy, immune function, inflammation, insulin sensitivity and cellular repair

1. Introduction

Fasting, an age-old practice with roots in religious, cultural, and health traditions, has recently gained scientific attention for its potential health benefits. Among these, its effects on immune function have sparked considerable interest. The immune system, a complex network of cells, tissues, and organs, is responsible for defending the body against harmful pathogens such as bacteria, viruses, and other foreign invaders. Maintaining a well-functioning immune system is essential for overall health and longevity. As such, understanding how various lifestyle factors, including diet and fasting, influence immune resilience has become a focal point of research [1].

In recent years, the exploration of fasting has moved beyond its traditional contexts, with modern science examining its biological effects in unprecedented detail. Fasting is generally defined as the voluntary abstention from food for a specific period, but it can take various forms. Intermittent fasting, for example, involves alternating periods of eating and fasting within a 24-hour cycle, while prolonged fasting refers to extended periods without food intake, sometimes lasting several days. Another popular approach is time-restricted feeding, where all meals are consumed within a narrow window of time, followed by a prolonged fasting period.

The physiological effects of fasting are profound and multifaceted. When the body enters a fasting state, several metabolic changes occur. Insulin levels drop, prompting the body to begin breaking down stored fat for energy. This shift in energy sources, from glucose to fatty acids and ketones, not only affects metabolism but also has significant implications for various biological processes, including immune function. One of the most intriguing aspects of fasting is its ability to induce autophagy, a cellular process that involves the degradation and recycling of damaged or dysfunctional cellular components. This process is crucial for maintaining cellular homeostasis and has been linked to the regulation of immune responses.

The immune system itself is broadly divided into two main branches: innate immunity and adaptive immunity. Innate immunity is the body's first line of defense and includes physical barriers like the skin, as well as immune cells such as macrophages, neutrophils, and natural killer (NK) cells. These components provide a non-specific response to pathogens, acting quickly to eliminate invaders. Adaptive immunity, on the other hand, is a more specialized system that targets specific pathogens [2]. This branch involves T cells and B cells, which are responsible for remembering and attacking specific antigens. Both arms of the immune system must function optimally to ensure overall health and resilience.

The relationship between fasting and the immune system is complex and involves several mechanisms. For instance, fasting has been shown to modulate inflammation, a key component of the immune response. Inflammation is a natural and necessary response to injury or infection, but chronic inflammation is associated with a range of health problems, including autoimmune diseases, cardiovascular conditions, and even cancer. Fasting appears to influence inflammation by affecting key signaling pathways, such as the NF-κB pathway, which regulates the expression of pro-inflammatory cytokines. By reducing the levels of these inflammatory markers, fasting may help prevent the immune system from becoming overactive, thereby reducing the risk of chronic diseases [1].

Another significant impact of fasting on immune function is related to immune cell production and regeneration. Research has shown that fasting can lead to a temporary reduction in white blood cell counts, particularly during prolonged fasting. However, this reduction is often followed by a rebound effect once normal eating is resumed. This cycle of reduction and regeneration is thought to rejuvenate the immune system, as fasting-induced autophagy helps eliminate older or damaged immune cells, making way for the production of new, more effective ones. This process could enhance the immune system's ability to respond to infections and other challenges.

Immunometabolism, the study of how metabolism regulates immune cell function, is another area where fasting has shown promise. Immune cells, like all cells, require energy to function, and their metabolic needs change depending on their activity level and the presence of pathogens. Fasting alters the metabolic environment of the body, shifting energy sources from glucose to fatty acids and ketones. This metabolic shift has been shown to affect immune cell function, potentially enhancing the efficiency of certain immune responses. For example, the production of ketones during fasting has been linked to improved T-cell function and reduced inflammation, suggesting that fasting could help optimize the immune system's response to pathogens [3].

In addition to its direct effects on immune cells and inflammation, fasting also appears to influence immune function through its impact on the gut microbiome. The gut microbiome is a complex community of microorganisms that reside in the digestive tract and play a crucial role in immune function. A healthy gut microbiome is essential for maintaining a robust immune system, as it helps regulate inflammation, supports the production of certain vitamins and metabolites, and even influences the development of immune cells. Fasting has been shown to lead to changes in the composition of the gut microbiome, increasing the abundance of beneficial bacteria and reducing harmful species. These changes may help modulate immune function, as a balanced gut microbiome is associated with better immune resilience and a lower risk of autoimmune diseases.

Despite the promising evidence supporting the benefits of fasting for immune function, it is important to recognize that the relationship between fasting and the immune system is not fully understood. The effects of fasting can vary depending on factors such as age, sex, overall health, and the specific fasting protocol used. For example, while intermittent fasting may be beneficial for some individuals, prolonged fasting could be detrimental, particularly for those with underlying health conditions or compromised immune systems. As such, more research is needed to fully elucidate the mechanisms through which fasting influences immune function and to determine the most effective fasting protocols for different populations [1, 2].

One of the most exciting areas of research in this field is the potential application of fasting in clinical settings. For instance, fasting has been proposed as a complementary therapy for cancer patients undergoing chemotherapy. Chemotherapy is known to suppress the immune system, leaving patients vulnerable to infections and other complications. Some studies suggest that fasting before chemotherapy can protect healthy cells from the toxic effects of the treatment while enhancing the effectiveness of the therapy against cancer cells. This concept, known as differential stress resistance, is based on the idea that healthy cells enter a protective mode during fasting, making them more resistant to stress, while cancer cells, which are often unable to adapt to the metabolic changes induced by fasting, become more vulnerable to treatment.

Furthermore, fasting may also have implications for autoimmune diseases, where the immune system mistakenly attacks the body's own tissues. By modulating inflammation and promoting immune cell regeneration, fasting could help restore balance to an overactive immune system, reducing the severity of autoimmune symptoms. However, this area of research is still in its early stages, and more studies are needed to determine the safety and efficacy of fasting as a treatment for autoimmune conditions [4].

In conclusion, fasting represents a fascinating intersection between nutrition and immune function, offering a potential strategy for enhancing immune resilience. Through mechanisms such as autophagy, inflammation modulation, and changes in immune cell metabolism, fasting has the potential to support a robust and adaptive immune system. However, as with any intervention, it is essential to approach fasting with an understanding of its complexities and to tailor it to individual needs and health conditions. While the current evidence is promising, further research is needed to fully understand the long-term effects of fasting on immune function and to develop personalized fasting protocols that optimize immune health. As research continues to uncover the intricate links between fasting and immune function, we may find new ways to harness this ancient practice for modern health challenges, potentially offering a valuable tool in the prevention and management of a wide range of diseases.

2. The immune system: An overview

Before diving into the specifics of fasting, it is crucial to understand the fundamental components of the immune system. The immune system is a complex network of cells, tissues, and organs that work in harmony to protect the body from pathogens, including bacteria, viruses, fungi, and parasites. It is broadly divided into two main branches:

Innate Immunity: The first line of defense, providing a non-specific response to pathogens. Key components include physical barriers like the skin and mucous membranes, as well as immune cells such as macrophages, neutrophils, and natural killer (NK) cells.

Adaptive Immunity: A more specialized system that targets specific pathogens. This branch involves T cells and B cells, which are responsible for remembering and attacking specific antigens [1, 5].

Both arms of the immune system must function optimally to ensure overall health and resilience. However, various factors, including diet, stress, and lifestyle, can modulate immune function, making the study of these influences critical.

3. Fasting: Types and physiological effects

Fasting, the practice of abstaining from food and sometimes drink for a period, has been a part of human culture for millennia. Its origins are rooted in religious and spiritual practices, but in recent years, fasting has gained popularity for its potential health benefits. Various fasting protocols have been studied for their effects on metabolism, aging, disease prevention, and overall health. Understanding the different types of fasting and their physiological effects can provide insights into how this practice influences the body and how it can be used to optimize health.

4. Types of fasting

Fasting can be categorized into several different types, each with unique characteristics and protocols. The most common forms of fasting include intermittent fasting, prolonged fasting, and time-restricted eating.

4.1 Intermittent fasting (IF)

Intermittent fasting is perhaps the most popular form of fasting in contemporary health and wellness circles. It involves cycling between periods of eating and fasting within a 24-hour period or over a week. There are several variations of intermittent fasting, including:

- *16/8 method:* This method involves fasting for 16 hours and eating all meals within an 8-hour window. For example, one might eat between 12:00 PM and 8:00 PM and fast from 8:00 PM to 12:00 PM the next day.

- *5:2 diet:* This approach involves eating normally for five days of the week and significantly reducing calorie intake (typically around 500–600 calories) on the other two non-consecutive days.

- *Eat-stop-eat:* This method involves a full 24-hour fast once or twice a week. For example, if you finish dinner at 7:00 PM on Monday, you would not eat again until 7:00 PM on Tuesday.

- *Alternate-day fasting:* As the name suggests, this method involves alternating between days of regular eating and days of fasting or eating very few calories (about 500 calories).

Intermittent fasting is praised for its flexibility and has been studied for its potential benefits in weight loss, metabolic health, and even longevity.

4.2 Prolonged fasting

Prolonged fasting typically refers to fasting periods that last longer than 24 hours, ranging from 48 hours to several days. This type of fasting is less common and is often done under medical supervision, especially when extended beyond three days. Prolonged fasting is more extreme than intermittent fasting and can lead to more pronounced physiological changes, including significant shifts in metabolism, enhanced autophagy, and changes in hormone levels.

Prolonged fasting is sometimes used in clinical settings or by individuals seeking to reset their metabolism, reduce inflammation, or explore the potential anti-aging effects of extended calorie restriction [3].

4.3 Time-restricted eating (TRE)

Time-restricted eating is a type of intermittent fasting where all daily caloric intake is confined to a specific window of time, typically between 4 to 12 hours. The most common pattern is an 8-hour eating window followed by a 16-hour fasting period (similar to the 16/8 method of intermittent fasting). TRE differs slightly from other forms of intermittent fasting in that it focuses strictly on the timing of meals rather than the quantity or caloric content.

TRE is often seen as a more sustainable approach to fasting, as it aligns with the body's natural circadian rhythms and can be easier to maintain over the long term.

5. Physiological effects of fasting

Fasting induces a variety of physiological changes in the body, many of which are linked to health benefits. These effects can vary depending on the type and duration of fasting, as well as individual factors such as age, sex, and baseline metabolic health. The following sections explore some of the key physiological effects of fasting.

5.1 Metabolic shift and ketosis

One of the most significant physiological effects of fasting is the shift in the body's energy metabolism. Under normal conditions, the body primarily relies on glucose (derived from carbohydrates) for energy. However, during fasting, when carbohydrate intake is limited or absent, the body is forced to find alternative energy sources.

After about 12–16 hours of fasting, glycogen stores in the liver and muscles become depleted, and the body begins to break down stored fat into fatty acids and ketone bodies, a process known as ketosis. Ketone bodies, particularly beta-hydroxybutyrate (BHB), become the primary energy source for the brain and other tissues during prolonged fasting.

This metabolic shift to ketosis has several implications for health:

- *Weight loss:* By tapping into fat stores for energy, fasting can promote fat loss, which is why it is often used as a strategy for weight management.

- *Insulin sensitivity:* Fasting has been shown to improve insulin sensitivity, which can lower the risk of type 2 diabetes and other metabolic disorders.

- *Mental clarity and focus:* Some people report improved cognitive function during fasting, which may be related to the brain's utilization of ketones as a more efficient energy source.

5.2 Hormonal changes

Fasting induces significant changes in the levels of various hormones, which can have wide-ranging effects on the body's physiology.

- *Insulin:* One of the most immediate effects of fasting is a decrease in insulin levels. Insulin is a hormone that facilitates the uptake of glucose into cells, and lower insulin levels during fasting help shift the body into fat burning mode. Reduced insulin levels are associated with improved metabolic health and a lower risk of insulin resistance.

- *Glucagon:* Glucagon is a hormone that works in opposition to insulin by promoting the release of glucose from liver stores. During fasting, glucagon levels rise, facilitating the mobilization of energy stores to maintain blood glucose levels.

- *Human growth hormone (HGH):* Fasting has been shown to increase the production of HGH, a hormone that plays a key role in growth, metabolism, and muscle preservation. Elevated HGH levels during fasting can help maintain muscle mass and promote fat burning.

- *Cortisol:* Cortisol, a stress hormone, may also increase during fasting, particularly in the early stages. While chronic elevation of cortisol is associated with negative health effects, the transient increase during fasting is part of the body's adaptive response to the absence of food.

5.3 Cellular autophagy

Autophagy is a cellular process where cells break down and recycle damaged or dysfunctional components. It is a crucial mechanism for maintaining cellular health and preventing the accumulation of harmful proteins and organelles that could contribute to diseases such as cancer and neurodegeneration.

Fasting is a potent inducer of autophagy. When nutrient intake is reduced, cells shift from growth and proliferation modes to maintenance and repair. This shift activates autophagy, allowing cells to clean up and renew themselves. The activation of autophagy during fasting is believed to contribute to many of the health benefits associated with the practice, including improved longevity, reduced inflammation, and enhanced resistance to stress [6].

5.4 Inflammation and immune function

Inflammation is a natural response to injury or infection, but chronic inflammation is a risk factor for many chronic diseases, including cardiovascular disease, diabetes, and cancer. Fasting has been shown to have anti-inflammatory effects, which may be mediated through several mechanisms:

- *Reduction of pro-inflammatory cytokines:* Fasting can lead to a decrease in the levels of pro-inflammatory cytokines, such as tumor necrosis factor-alpha (TNF-α) and interleukin-6 (IL-6). These cytokines play a role in the development of chronic inflammation and are linked to various inflammatory diseases.

- *Enhanced immune cell function:* Fasting has been found to improve the function of certain immune cells, such as macrophages and natural killer (NK) cells. It also promotes the regeneration of immune cells through the induction of autophagy, which helps eliminate damaged or aged immune cells and replaces them with new, more effective ones.

- *Impact on the gut microbiome:* The gut microbiome plays a crucial role in regulating inflammation and immune function. Fasting has been shown to alter the composition of the gut microbiome in ways that may reduce inflammation and enhance immune resilience.

5.5 Cardiovascular health

Fasting has several effects on cardiovascular health, which can contribute to a lower risk of heart disease. Some of these effects include:

- *Improved blood lipid profile:* Fasting has been shown to reduce levels of total cholesterol, low-density lipoprotein (LDL) cholesterol, and triglycerides, all of which are risk factors for cardiovascular disease. It may also increase levels of high-density lipoprotein (HDL) cholesterol, which is protective against heart disease.

- *Lower blood pressure:* Fasting can lead to reductions in blood pressure, which is a major risk factor for cardiovascular disease. This effect is likely due to a combination of factors, including weight loss, improved insulin sensitivity, and reduced inflammation.

- *Reduced oxidative stress:* Oxidative stress, caused by an imbalance between free radicals and antioxidants, plays a role in the development of cardiovascular disease. Fasting has been shown to reduce oxidative stress by enhancing the body's antioxidant defenses and reducing the production of reactive oxygen species (ROS).

5.6 Longevity and aging

The potential for fasting to extend lifespan and delay the onset of age-related diseases is one of the most exciting areas of research. Studies in animals have shown that calorie restriction, a form of fasting, can extend lifespan and improve health span—the period of life spent in good health.

Fasting may promote longevity through several mechanisms:

- *Enhanced autophagy and cellular maintenance:* By promoting autophagy, fasting helps maintain cellular health and prevent the accumulation of damaged components that contribute to aging.

- *Hormetic stress:* Fasting introduces a mild stress to the body, which activates protective pathways and increases the body's resilience to more severe stresses. This process, known as hormesis, is thought to play a role in the health benefits of fasting.

- *Reduced risk of chronic diseases:* By improving metabolic health, reducing inflammation, and enhancing immune function, fasting may lower the risk of chronic diseases that are major contributors to aging and mortality.

5.7 Cognitive function and brain health

Fasting has been shown to have positive effects on brain health and cognitive function. These effects are likely due to a combination of metabolic changes, enhanced autophagy, and reduced inflammation.

- *Neuroprotection:* Fasting may protect the brain from neurodegenerative diseases by reducing oxidative stress, inflammation, and the accumulation of toxic proteins that are characteristic of conditions like Alzheimer's disease.

- *Enhanced neuroplasticity:* Fasting has been shown to increase the production of brain-derived neurotrophic factor (BDNF), a protein that supports the growth and survival of neurons. Increased BDNF levels are associated with improved learning, memory, and cognitive function.

- *Improved mental clarity:* Many people report improved mental clarity and focus during fasting, which may be related to the brain's utilization of ketones as an energy source and the reduction in blood glucose fluctuations.

6. The impact of fasting on immune function

Fasting has long been practiced for various reasons, including religious observance, cultural traditions, and health benefits. In recent years, the scientific community has begun to explore fasting not just as a weight management tool but as a practice that may have profound effects on various physiological systems, including the immune system. The immune system is a complex network that protects the body against infections, cancers, and other diseases. Understanding how fasting interacts with this system can provide insights into potential therapeutic strategies for enhancing immune function and overall health. This chapter will delve into the multifaceted effects of fasting on immune function, exploring the underlying biological mechanisms, the impact on different immune cells, the role of autophagy, inflammation, and immunometabolism, as well as the implications for clinical applications [7].

7. Fasting and the immune system: A complex relationship

Fasting is characterized by the voluntary abstention from food intake for varying periods, leading to several metabolic shifts in the body. These shifts are not only relevant to energy balance but also significantly impact the immune system. The immune system is broadly categorized into two components: innate immunity, which provides immediate but non-specific responses to pathogens, and adaptive immunity, which is slower but highly specific and involves the development of immunological memory. Both components must work in harmony to protect the body effectively, and both are influenced by fasting.

During fasting, the body undergoes a transition from utilizing glucose as its primary energy source to relying more on fatty acids and ketones. This metabolic shift has been shown to influence immune cell function, as immune cells have specific metabolic requirements that change depending on their state of activation or quiescence. The interplay between fasting-induced metabolic changes and immune function is complex and involves several key mechanisms.

8. Autophagy: The cellular cleanup process

One of the most significant effects of fasting on the immune system is the activation of autophagy, a catabolic process where cells degrade and recycle their components. Autophagy plays a critical role in maintaining cellular homeostasis by removing damaged organelles, misfolded proteins, and pathogens from the cell. This process is essential for the optimal functioning of immune cells, particularly in the context of responding to infections.

During fasting, autophagy is upregulated, which has several implications for immune function. For instance, enhanced autophagy can lead to improved antigen presentation, a process where immune cells display pieces of pathogens (antigens) on their surfaces to T cells. This presentation is crucial for the activation of adaptive immune responses. By improving antigen presentation, fasting can potentially enhance the body's ability to recognize and combat pathogens more effectively.

Moreover, autophagy is involved in the regulation of inflammation, another key aspect of immune function. Inflammation is the body's response to injury or infection, characterized by the release of pro-inflammatory cytokines and the recruitment of immune cells to the site of damage or infection. While acute inflammation is protective, chronic inflammation can be detrimental and is associated with various diseases, including autoimmune disorders, cardiovascular diseases, and cancer. Fasting-induced autophagy has been shown to help resolve inflammation by promoting the clearance of inflammatory mediators and damaged cells, thereby restoring tissue homeostasis [2, 7].

9. Inflammation and immune modulation

Fasting has a notable impact on inflammation, a critical component of the immune response. Inflammation is a double-edged sword; while it is necessary for defending the body against infections and promoting healing, excessive or chronic inflammation can contribute to the development of numerous diseases. Fasting appears to modulate inflammation in a way that balances the body's immune responses, reducing the risk of chronic inflammatory conditions.

One of the primary mechanisms through which fasting influences inflammation is the modulation of key signaling pathways, such as the nuclear factor kappa-light-chain-enhancer of activated B cells (NF-κB) pathway. NF-κB is a protein complex that controls the transcription of DNA and the production of pro-inflammatory cytokines. Under normal circumstances, NF-κB is kept in an inactive state in the cytoplasm of cells. However, in response to stimuli such as infections or stress, NF-κB is activated and translocates to the nucleus, where it initiates the expression of inflammatory genes [8].

Fasting has been shown to inhibit the activation of NF-κB, thereby reducing the production of pro-inflammatory cytokines such as tumor necrosis factor-alpha (TNF-α), interleukin-6 (IL-6), and interleukin-1 beta (IL-1β). By dampening the inflammatory response, fasting may help prevent the immune system from becoming overactive, which is a common feature of autoimmune diseases. Additionally, reduced levels of systemic inflammation are associated with improved overall health and a lower risk of developing chronic diseases.

10. Fasting and immune cell function

Fasting affects the production, function, and lifespan of various immune cells, including lymphocytes, neutrophils, macrophages, and natural killer (NK) cells. Each of these cell types plays a unique role in the immune response, and fasting can influence their activity in different ways.

Lymphocytes, which include T cells and B cells, are central to the adaptive immune response. Fasting has been shown to cause a temporary reduction in the number of circulating lymphocytes, particularly during prolonged fasting. This reduction is often followed by a compensatory increase in lymphocyte production once normal feeding resumes. This cycle of reduction and regeneration is thought to contribute to the rejuvenation of the immune system, as it may help eliminate older or damaged immune cells and promote the generation of new, more effective ones. Furthermore, fasting-induced metabolic changes, such as increased ketone production, have been shown to enhance T cell function, potentially improving the body's ability to respond to infections and other immune challenges.

Neutrophils are the most abundant type of white blood cells and play a critical role in the innate immune response by rapidly responding to infections. Fasting has been found to influence neutrophil activity, with some studies suggesting that short-term fasting may enhance neutrophil function, potentially improving the body's initial response to infections. However, the effects of prolonged fasting on neutrophils are less clear and may depend on the context, such as the presence of underlying health conditions [9].

Macrophages are versatile immune cells that play a dual role in the immune response: they are involved in both the detection and destruction of pathogens and the resolution of inflammation and tissue repair. Fasting has been shown to alter macrophage polarization, the process by which macrophages adopt different functional states depending on the signals they receive from their environment. For example, fasting may promote the polarization of macrophages toward an anti-inflammatory state (known as the M2 phenotype), which supports tissue repair and the resolution of inflammation. This shift in macrophage function could be beneficial in preventing chronic inflammation and promoting healing.

Natural killer (NK) cells are another crucial component of the innate immune system, responsible for identifying and destroying infected or cancerous cells. Fasting has been shown to influence NK cell activity, with some studies suggesting that short-term fasting may enhance NK cell function, potentially improving the body's ability to detect and eliminate abnormal cells. However, the long-term effects of fasting on NK cell activity require further investigation [9].

11. Immunometabolism: The intersection of metabolism and immune function

Immunometabolism is an emerging field that explores the interplay between metabolic processes and immune cell function. Immune cells, like all cells, require energy to perform their functions, and their metabolic needs change depending on their state of activation. Fasting, by altering the body's metabolic environment, can have a profound impact on immunometabolism and, consequently, immune function.

During fasting, the body shifts from using glucose as its primary energy source to relying more on fatty acids and ketones. This metabolic shift is significant for immune cells, which must adapt to these changes in nutrient availability. For instance, activated T cells, which are crucial for the adaptive immune response, typically rely on glucose to meet their energy demands. However, during fasting, these cells must adapt to using fatty acids and ketones as alternative energy sources. This adaptation may influence T cell function and the overall immune response.

Ketones, which are produced during fasting as a result of increased fat metabolism, have been shown to have anti-inflammatory effects. One of the key ketones, β-hydroxybutyrate (BHB), has been found to inhibit the activation of the NLRP3 inflammasome, a multiprotein complex that plays a critical role in the production of pro-inflammatory cytokines. By inhibiting the NLRP3 inflammasome, BHB may help reduce inflammation and protect against chronic inflammatory diseases [5].

Additionally, the metabolic environment created by fasting may influence the differentiation and function of immune cells. For example, the balance between different T cell subsets, such as pro-inflammatory Th17 cells and regulatory T cells (Tregs), can be affected by changes in metabolic pathways. Fasting has been shown to promote the differentiation of Tregs, which play a crucial role in maintaining immune tolerance and preventing autoimmune diseases. This shift in T cell balance could be one of the ways fasting helps modulate the immune response and prevent excessive inflammation.

12. The gut microbiome: A mediator of Fasting's immune effects

The gut microbiome, a complex community of microorganisms residing in the digestive tract, plays a crucial role in regulating immune function. The composition of the gut microbiome can influence everything from inflammation to the development of autoimmune diseases. Fasting has been shown to impact the gut microbiome in ways that may enhance immune resilience.

During fasting, changes in diet and nutrient availability can lead to shifts in the composition of the gut microbiome. For example, fasting has been associated with an increase in the abundance of beneficial bacteria, such as those belonging to the genera Lactobacillus and Bifidobacterium. These bacteria are known to produce short-chain fatty acids (SCFAs), which have anti-inflammatory properties and can help maintain the integrity of the gut barrier, preventing the leakage of harmful substances into the bloodstream.

Furthermore, fasting may reduce the abundance of pathogenic bacteria and promote the growth of microbes that are associated with better metabolic health. These changes in the gut microbiome could have downstream effects on the immune system, potentially reducing inflammation and enhancing immune tolerance. Additionally, a balanced gut microbiome is associated with improved production of metabolites that support immune function, such as SCFAs and other signaling molecules that regulate immune cell activity [4].

13. Clinical implications: Fasting as a therapeutic strategy

The impact of fasting on immune function has significant implications for clinical applications. One area of interest is the potential use of fasting as an adjunct therapy in cancer treatment. Cancer and its treatments, such as chemotherapy and radiation, can have profound effects on the immune system, often leading to immunosuppression and increased susceptibility to infections. Some studies suggest that fasting before chemotherapy can protect healthy cells from the toxic effects of treatment while making cancer cells more vulnerable to destruction, a concept known as differential stress resistance.

Fasting may also have applications in the management of autoimmune diseases, where the immune system mistakenly attacks the body's own tissues. By modulating inflammation and promoting immune cell regeneration, fasting could help restore balance to an overactive immune system and reduce the severity of autoimmune symptoms. However, this area of research is still in its early stages, and more studies are needed to determine the safety and efficacy of fasting as a treatment for autoimmune conditions [10].

In addition to its potential therapeutic applications, fasting could also be used as a preventive strategy to enhance immune resilience and reduce the risk of chronic diseases. By promoting autophagy, modulating inflammation, and influencing the gut microbiome, fasting may help support a robust and adaptive immune system, capable of responding effectively to infections and other immune challenges.

14. Conclusion

Fasting represents a powerful tool that can influence immune function in multiple ways. Through mechanisms such as autophagy, modulation of inflammation, and changes in immune cell metabolism, fasting has the potential to enhance immune resilience and support overall health. However, it is essential to approach fasting with an understanding of its complexities and to tailor it to individual needs and health conditions. While the current evidence is promising, further research is needed to fully understand the long-term effects of fasting on immune function and to develop personalized fasting protocols that optimize immune health. As research continues to uncover the intricate links between fasting and immune function, we may find new ways to harness this ancient practice for modern health challenges, offering a valuable tool in the prevention and management of a wide range of diseases.

Acknowledgements

I would like to express my sincere gratitude to all those who contributed to the successful completion of this book chapter.

First and foremost, I extend my heartfelt thanks to our esteemed Head of Department, Dr. Archana Dhok, whose invaluable guidance, support, and leadership have been instrumental throughout this journey. Your encouragement has been a constant source of motivation.

I am deeply grateful to Dr. Ashish Anjankar, Dr. Ranjit Ambad, Dr. Meghali Kaple, Dr. Anjali Bagga, Dr. Roshan Kumar Jha whose expertise and insights greatly enriched this work. Your constructive feedback and scholarly advice have helped shape the content and improve its quality.

I would also like to acknowledge the contributions of my fellow teaching staff members, who have offered their support and collaboration at every stage. Your discussions and shared experiences have provided me with a broader perspective on the subject matter.

A special thanks to the postgraduate students, whose enthusiasm and inquisitiveness inspired me to explore new ideas and delve deeper into the topic. Your passion for learning has been a driving force behind this chapter's development.

Additionally, I wish to recognize the non-teaching staff, whose logistical and administrative support made this process much smoother. Your dedication to ensuring that everything runs efficiently is greatly appreciated.

Finally, I thank my family and friends for their unwavering support and encouragement during this endeavor.

Conflict of interest

The authors declare no conflict of interest.

Author details

Rakesh Kumar Jha* and Ankita Kondhalkar
Jawaharlal Nehru Medical College, Datta Meghe Institute of Higher Education and Research (DMIHER), Sawangi (Meghe), Wardha, Maharashtra, India

*Address all correspondence to: jhaarakesh1993@gmail.com

References

[1] Longo VD, Mattson MP. Fasting: Molecular mechanisms and clinical applications. Cell Metabolism. 2014;**19**(2):181-192. DOI: 10.1016/j.cmet.2013.12.008

[2] Mattson MP, Longo VD, Harvie M. Impact of intermittent fasting on health and disease processes. Ageing Research Reviews. 2017;**39**:46-58. DOI: 10.1016/j.arr.2016.10.005

[3] Anton SD, Moehl K, Donahoo WT, Marosi K, Lee SA, Mainous AG, et al. Flipping the metabolic switch: Understanding and applying the health benefits of fasting. Obesity. 2018;**26**(2):254-268. DOI: 10.1002/oby.22065

[4] Brandhorst S, Choi IY, Wei M, et al. A periodic diet that mimics fasting promotes multi-system regeneration, enhanced cognitive performance, and healthspan. Cell Metabolism. 2015;**22**(1):86-99. DOI: 10.1016/j.cmet.2015.05.012

[5] Patterson RE, Laughlin GA, LaCroix AZ, Hartman SJ, Natarajan L, Senger CM, et al. Intermittent fasting and human metabolic health. Journal of the Academy of Nutrition and Dietetics. 2015;**115**(8):1203-1212. DOI: 10.1016/j.jand.2015.02.018

[6] de Cabo R, Mattson MP. Effects of intermittent fasting on health, aging, and disease. The New England Journal of Medicine. 2019;**381**(26):2541-2551. DOI: 10.1056/NEJMra1905136

[7] Barzilai N, Bartke A. Genetic and dietary connections: Studies of aging in mice. Science. 2009;**326**(5950):653-654. DOI: 10.1126/science.1177371

[8] Ahmet I, Wan R, Mattson MP, Lakatta EG, Talan M. Cardioprotection by intermittent fasting in rats. Circulation. 2005;**112**(20):3115-3121. DOI: 10.1161/CIRCULATIONAHA.105.554667

[9] Halberg N, Henriksen M, Söderhamn N, Stallknecht B, Ploug T, Schjerling P, et al. Effect of intermittent fasting and refeeding on insulin action in healthy men. Journal of Applied Physiology. 2005;**99**(6):2128-2136. DOI: 10.1152/japplphysiol.00683.2005

[10] Lee C, Longo VD. Fasting vs dietary restriction in cellular protection and cancer treatment: From model organisms to patients. Oncogene. 2011;**30**(30):3305-3316. DOI: 10.1038/onc.2011.91

Chapter 5

Fasting and Autophagy and Its Effect on Health

Ying Yang

Abstract

Intermittent fasting, a cleansing activity that severely restricts calorie intake, is an effective means of activating autophagy. As a dietary pattern, intermittent fasting can delay aging and reduce the risk of age-related diseases. Intermittent fasting helps maintain the homeostasis of the body through a series of hormonal and metabolic changes, protecting a variety of metabolic diseases and preventing a variety of chronic diseases. And it has been shown to improve the efficacy of weight loss and obesity-related non-alcoholic fatty liver disease and a variety of health indicators. There are still some challenges in the area of intermittent fasting's health effects, and further long-term clinical studies are still needed.

Keywords: fasting, autophagy, metabolic, aging, liver rhythm

1. Introduction

Organisms have evolved adaptive responses to fight hunger in order to survive for thousands of years. The past century has seen a shift from diseases caused by inadequate nutrient supply to overnutrition, leading to obesity, diabetes, and cardiovascular diseases, which promote the application of fasting strategies [1]. Intermittent fasting (IF) is a practice of severely restricting calorie intake during the day, in which an individual eats repeatedly for a period of time (e.g., 16–48 hours). IF lasts from 2 to 21 days or more and intermittently eliminates the intake of consecutive meals or one meal, rather than reducing meal size. IF has beneficial effects on many different health indicators [2]. IF can reduce the risk of age-related diseases. Studies of IF and time-restricted feeding (limiting food intake to less than 8 hours per day) have shown efficacy in weight loss and improvements in multiple health measures, including reductions in insulin resistance and cardiovascular disease risk factors [2].

There is already substantial evidence that IF may help prevent chronic diseases such as high blood pressure, metabolic syndromes (such as diabetes, cardiovascular and neurological diseases), asthma, chronic pain syndromes, rheumatic diseases, cancers, and heart disease, as well as delay or prevent chronic inflammatory and most chronic degenerative diseases. When mice are given a low-calorie, low-protein fasting simulated diet, inflammation, memory, and immune aging of aging mice are improved, and their life span is extended. More long-term human studies are needed to elaborate on the effects of fasting on metabolism, aging, and life span [3]. The mechanisms by which fasting promotes health include, for example, autophagy promotion, neuroendocrine activation induced by fasting, reduced mitochondrial oxidative stress, the increased expression of neurotrophic factors, and a general decline in signals associated with aging [4–6].

Autophagy recycles depleted substances and treats damaged organelles by lysosomal degradation. In addition, lysosomes are central regulators of fasting responses and cellular metabolism, storing nutrients in lysosomes that are released during starvation. Lysosomes direct cellular processes to obtain the beneficial effects of IF and restore homeostasis during feasts and famines [1].

IF involves a series of synergistic hormonal and metabolic changes to maintain the body's cell homeostasis and metabolic balance and has shown a good protective effect against various metabolic diseases [7]. Stratton et al. studied physiological responses (autophagy changes, hormonal environment in the body, energy expenditure, and substrate metabolism) that occur throughout acute fasting. Fasting regimens of >18 hours and <18 hours may produce different longitudinal outcomes. And a deeper understanding of the multiple physiological responses caused by fasting duration is needed to significantly improve the precise selection of fasting regimens for specific populations [8]. In animal and human studies, IF has been shown to have many health benefits including critical illness, with beneficial effects based on multiple metabolic and endocrine changes [9]. Preliminary studies have reported that time-restricted feeding improves cardiometabolic health in rodents and humans [10]. Metabolic indicators that can be improved include cardiometabolic parameters (cholesterol, blood pressure, and triglyceride levels) [11]. IF may be beneficial for the management of non-alcoholic fatty liver disease (NAFLD), which is associated with obesity [12]. Iulia Minciuna et al. made a review to discuss the effect of IF on improving the prognosis of NASH disease and the main pathogenesis metabolic drivers and summarized the current clinical evidence [11].

IF as a diet helps prevent a variety of chronic diseases and delay aging, through a series of hormonal and metabolic changes to maintain the homeostasis of the body to protect a variety of metabolic diseases. Autophagy-lysosomes regulate the fasting response to achieve homeostasis. The following sections describe the role of IF in the brain, heart, liver, gallbladder, metabolism, aging, infection, immunity, cancer, circadian rhythms. Finally, some challenges and future research directions of IF are summarized.

2. Brain

2.1 Depression and high-fat diet

Igwe and his colleagues reviewed the neurobiological mechanisms that might be involved in IF. The contributing factors include autophagy, reactive oxygen species, cyclic adenosine phosphate reaction element binding protein, ketone bodies, free fatty acids, neurotransmitters, orexin, brain-derived neurotrophic factor, cytokines, leptin, and auxin-releasing peptides, some of which are potential factors for improving symptoms of depression [13]. In high-fat diet rats, IF can improve cerebellar structure and morphology, improve metabolic syndrome, and reduce body weight. The mechanism of fasting may be related to the restoration of autophagy destruction, inhibition of inflammation, and attenuation of oxidative stress [14].

2.2 Improve cognition and delay aging

Neurodegenerative diseases caused by aging are an increasingly significant global health problem. There are currently no drugs to treat neurodegenerative diseases, so there is an urgent need to develop prevention strategies/approaches. IF is considered an effective strategy for extending healthy life and longevity, but it is difficult to strictly follow these routines, which has led to the development of caloric restriction simulators [15]. Some animal models found that IF can reduce oxidative stress, improve cognition, and delay aging [16]. Sudasinghe et al. observed the effects of IF on neuroprotection against molecular markers of protein synthesis, autophagy, and antioxidant expression in animal models. IF significantly impaired protein synthesis only in the cortex. IF increases the expression of antioxidant oxidase (SOD2) in the cortex, but decreases the expression of antioxidant oxidase in the hippocampus with its high antioxidant content, which deserves more research [17].

The autophagy pathway is essential for the homeostasis of adult organisms and cells for long term, and it is often activated during stress periods. IF plays an important role in several progressive neurological diseases associated with accumulating cytotoxic peptides and protein aggregates. Ratliff et al. found that fruit flies treated with IF also had lower neural aggregation characteristics, and maintained a longer life span and more young behavior [18]. Brain regions are under specific protection from long-term IF. Neuronal death is due to increased amyloid β-induced toxicity, but autophagy is enhanced mediated by functional macromolecules and molecular chaperones. Autophagy has been shown to help clear Aβ peptide. And IF is a very promising treatment strategy at all stages of AD-related pathologic progression [19]. Huntington's disease is a neurodegenerative disease whose remission treatment is still difficult to achieve, and new therapeutic approaches including lifestyle changes need to be explored [20]. Huntington's disease is caused by the expression of Huntington's mutants. And the clearance rate of Huntington's mutants can be improved by gradually increasing the enzyme activity through the dietary rules that promote autophagy [21].

2.3 Brain injury

Numerous results have shown that several types of IF/caloric restriction promote recovery from traumatic brain injury. Recent studies have shown that various IF and caloric restriction programs can play a neuroprotective role in traumatic brain injury through multiple mechanisms, including reducing mitochondrial dysfunction, targeting apoptosis and autophagy, inhibiting glial cell response, promoting hippocampal neurogenesis, and shaping neural cell plasticity [22].

Not only does caloric restriction-induced autophagy have a neuroprotective effect on cerebral ischemia, but IF also has a protective effect, which can reduce infarct size and cerebral edema in focal cerebral ischemia models. IF improves neurobehavioral defects, reduces neuronal apoptosis, and saves neuronal loss. These neuroprotective mechanisms are partly due to the minimization of autophagy flux perturbations and the inhibition of apoptosis [23]. There is no satisfactory treatment for spinal cord injury, and its pathophysiology is complex and unclear, which is one of the leading causes of neurological dysfunction and death. IF has therapeutic value in making neurons survive after acute spinal cord injury in rats, and the underlying mechanism is related to the up-regulation of autophagy. Therefore, dietary intervention is a potential treatment [24].

3. The heart

3.1 Cardiac homeostasis and cardiometabolism

IF may reduce age-related cardiovascular disease [25]. Cardiometabolic disease remains a leading cause of death worldwide and can be prevented with lifestyle interventions. The dietary restriction programs including calorie restriction and IF have been shown to delay cardiovascular aging and promote health in animal models of cardiometabolic diseases. The related mechanisms include improved autophagy, mitochondrial dysfunction, inflammation, and oxidative stress [26]. Acute fasting activates autophagy, which is essential for cardiac homeostasis during fasting. Both animal and human studies have shown that IF and chronic caloric restriction extend life span, reduce risk factors for inflammatory and cardiometabolic diseases, reduce myocardial tissue damage, and activate cardioprotective metabolic programs [1]. One form of IF is time-restricted eating, which involves a longer daily fasting period. The time-restricted eating increases autophagy and has anti-aging effects on the human body. It can improve 24-hour blood sugar levels, change circadian clock gene expression, affect lipid metabolism, and influence the diurnal pattern of cortisol [10].

3.2 Myocardial infarction

IF can partially prevent acute myocardial infarction in elderly rats by reducing age-related changes in obesity, dyslipidemia, and diabetes. And IF is a dietary lifestyle that reduces the susceptibility of the elderly to acute myocardial infarction [25]. IF chronically activates cardiac and pancreatic autophagy to alleviate acute myocardial infarction in elderly rats [27]. Fasting effectively stimulates autophagy in the myocardium, maintains cardiac function during long-term starvation, and plays a beneficial role in myocardial ischemia-reperfusion injury after acute myocardial infarction [28].

3.3 Cardiotoxicity caused by antibiotics

Anthracyclines such as doxorubicin cause cardiotoxicity and associated autophagy damage. It has been found that IF increases doxorubicin-associated mortality and cardiomyopathies by stimulating the autophagolysosomal transcription regulator, the transcription factor EB (TFEB). The safety of anthracyclines is noteworthy [29].

Doxorubicin is an effective anti-cancer drug with severe cardiotoxicity. IF has cardioprotective effects on cardiotoxicity mediated by doxorubicin by restoring autophagy, restoring oxidation state, alleviating apoptosis, and preserving cells. And IF can be used as a potential prevention and treatment method for doxorubicin cardiotoxicity [30].

4. Liver

4.1 Physiology and pathology

A better understanding of IF effects on autophagy in the liver may lead to new ways to combat liver disease. The effect on liver autophagy could lead to new ways to prevent and treat liver disease. Chaudhary et al. investigated the effects of IF on markers of autophagy in liver and skeletal muscle in mice and humans. Mice fed both food and high-fat diets responded to IF, increasing autophagy markers in the liver. Fasting also increased autophagy markers (LAMP1 protein and Beclin1) mRNA levels in the liver of food-fed mice, while the markers in muscle did not change. It may be a response to weight loss [31]. The activation of liver autophagy by IF is very important for maintaining energy balance and cell homeostasis, cell and tissue remodeling, quality control, and defense against extracellular damage and pathogens. Liver autophagy is affected by various pathways and molecular mechanisms, such as energy, oxygen-free radical metabolism, and cellular stress response system, which can protect liver cells from environmental factors and genetic influences. These pathways stimulate the pro-inflammatory cytokines (interleukin-6 and tumor necrosis factor α), reducing the expression of aging-related molecules and preventing the development of liver tumors. By activating liver autophagy, IF has the potential to treat various liver diseases, including NAFLD, viral hepatitis, liver fibrosis, hepatocellular carcinoma, and drug-induced liver injury [6].

Semenovich et al. investigated the effects of IF and dietary restriction on liver injury induced by common bile duct ligation in rats, with special attention to changes in antioxidant-protective enzyme activity and energy metabolism. The diets of the included group of choledochal ligation rats included a voluntary diet for 1 month, IF, or 35% dietary restriction. The results showed that dietary restriction resulted in an increase in autophagy activation, antioxidant capacity, and glucose heterobiosis. However, dietary restriction was only used for preconditioning protection. For severe damage to cholestasis and oxidative stress, dietary restriction was not protective [32].

4.2 Non-alcoholic fatty liver

Non-alcoholic steatohepatitis may progress to end-stage liver disease and HCC without cirrhosis. NAFLD is a fatty liver disease that can lead to severe liver disease and is one of the most common chronic liver diseases. Currently, there are no approved effective drugs for NAFLD treatment, but it has been recognized that dietary changes and physical exercise are the basis for managing NAFLD [33]. A high-fat diet with high fructose is one of the main causes of NAFLD, and the mechanisms of action include β-oxidation of liver cells or impaired apolipoprotein secretion. A variety of regimens of IF have positive effects in both humans and animals, with potential efficacy in treating NAFLD [33]. Lavallee et al. reviewed and summarized the factors, protocols, evidence, and potential mechanisms of action actually considered in the clinical practice of IF in the treatment of NAFLD, including autophagy, intestinal microbiome, regulation of circadian rhythm, adipose tissue, and adipokines [12].

IF can significantly induce hepatocyte autophagy and improve the changes in liver structure and function caused by NAFLD. And the activation of hepatocyte autophagy is a method to treat liver complications [34]. Patients with NAFLD achieve weight control through short-term IF, while long-term IF (4-month alternate-day fasting) in healthy mice has effects on systemic and liver lipid metabolism, manifested as a significant increase in liver autophagy, excessive accumulation of liver triglycerides, and a significant decrease in liver mTOR phosphorylation [35]. Data from preclinical and clinical trials show that IF not only has positive benefits in activating autophagy, but also in alleviating metabolic disorders, resetting circadian rhythm, and promoting Browning of white tissues [33]. Both IF and switching to a normal diet improved the lipid deposition and metabolic disorder in NAFLD mice for 10 weeks and reduced the increase of body weight, liver weight, insulin resistance index, and activated autophagy and apoptosis in mice, but the efficacy of IF was superior to that of normal diet [36].

5. Metabolism

5.1 Weight and muscle mass

Patients with obesity and its related metabolic diseases require long-term weight control, and an in-depth understanding of weight loss interventions is necessary. Liu et al. proved that IF, exercise, and adjustment of daily diet to normal diet have similar effects on weight loss, but they have significantly different effects on metabolic status, etc. IF significantly affects genes involved in mitochondrial autophagy and autophagy, and core genes involved in butyric acid metabolism in the liver. However, the normal diet failed to improve metabolic homeostasis in obese mice [37]. However, the study by Wang et al. found that IF is better than exercise in controlling rat weight. For example, for skeletal muscle autophagy activation, the 14-day intervention time required for IF is shorter than the 28-day aerobic exercise time [38].

Yoshii et al. found that nutritional supplementation during fasting could regulate protein breakdown and synthesis, maintain skeletal muscle mass, and reduce body fat [39]. Zhang et al. found that arginine catabolic metabolism is an easy process to activate autophagy, which can be used to treat obesity and its complications [40].

5.2 Diabetes

Type 2 diabetes mellitus is one of the public health diseases in the world and deserves to be promoted by improving individual lifestyles to prevent onset and progression. IF has been shown to have a positive effect on Type 2 diabetes mellitus, reducing body weight and improving blood glucose. It can induce tissue-specific metabolic adaptation by increasing peripheral tissue autophagy, and improve autophagy in humans and obese mice. IF triggers metabolic transformation to improve systemic metabolism by altering gut microbiota, adipose tissue remodeling, and correcting circadian rhythm disturbances. However, the mechanisms behind leaner diabetic individuals are not fully understood. However, IF protocol needs to monitor blood glucose and adjust drugs in time in clinical application because of the risk of hypoglycemia due to its safety and effectiveness [41]. Early symptoms of polyuria in diabetic nephropathy lead to dehydration in diabetic patients, and IF reduces polyuria by improving blood glucose status, although autophagy stimulation does not regulate the expression of renal aquaporin 2 in the disease [42]. Autophagy has a pathological effect on the submandibular gland and parotid gland of diabetic rats. And IF has a significant improvement effect [43]. The molecular mechanism of IF to improve type 2 diabetes is not only to improve liver function, functional β cell mass, and adipose tissue function in mice by enhancing autophagy and reducing oxidation and ER stress [44].

6. Aging

6.1 Life span

The burden of disease is greater in old age, including chronic diseases such as neurodegenerative diseases. In laboratory rats and mice, IF has far-reaching beneficial effects on many different health indicators and in many age-related diseases (including diabetes, cancers, cardiovascular disease and neurological disorders, such as Parkinson's disease, Alzheimer's disease, and stroke) [2].

IF has beneficial effects on the liver of elderly male albino rats, and its mechanisms include regulation of autophagy, as well as anti-inflammatory and anti-apoptotic effects on aging hepatocytes. IF may represent a safe, cheap, and simple method to improve the aging liver [45].

Pharmacological interventions prevent age-related diseases, and popular lifestyle interventions (such as IF and caloric restriction) induce autophagy and TFEB. Several new findings suggest that TFEB activity influences markers of aging, including inducing cell clearance and autophagy to promote protein homeostasis, inhibiting aging and promoting cell regeneration, inhibiting DNA damage and epigenetic modification, regulating pro-inflammatory and anti-inflammatory pathways, regulating mitochondrial quality control, and linking energy metabolism to nutrient sensing [46].

Although prolonged caloric restriction stimulates the death of type II autophagy cells and the resulting autophagy response is harmful, there is evidence that IF or caloric restriction can extend the life span of eukaryotic cells by inducing adaptive autophagy [7]. Compared to more stringent fasting regimens such as IF, regular fasting, and long-term caloric restriction, the simulated fasting diet is well tolerated in a clinical setting because it is a plant-based, low-protein, low-sugar diet regimen that is administered for 4 days in a 2-week cycle. The results show that feeding time and diet structure play an important role in a healthy life span [47].

6.2 Signals

Time-restricted eating (TRE) is one of intermittent fasting which is popular. The healthy life span of preclinical models of obesity is extended when TRE is given. Because miRNA is dysregulated in metabolic disorders of obesity, the specific mechanism may be through affecting the expression of circulating miRNA in intercellular communication factors. Full transcriptome miRNA assay was used to determine the expression difference of 14 miRNAs of 2083 human miRNAs before and after the TRE regimen. Down-regulation of miRNA targets is associated with autophagy (cell homeostasis and survival), Ras signaling (cell growth and proliferation), and insulin signaling (glucose uptake). Therefore, TRE protocol down-regulation of miRNA, which thereby inhibits cell growth pathways and activates cell survival pathways, may promote healthy aging [48].

7. Infection

There is currently no specific medicine for COVID-19. And maintaining a healthy life and boosting your immunity are the best ways to beat the disease. Healthy living is used in some clinical settings with IF to promote multiple health benefits, including activation of autophagy, a cellular surveillance system that enhances immunity. IF may constitute a promising COVID-19 prevention approach and may also be a potential strategy to combat SARS-CoV-2 infection [49].

The dawn-to-sunset fast is an intermittent fast commonly practiced during Ramadan. Dawn and sunset are two time zones that play a crucial role in the human circadian rhythm. The practice of dawn-to-sunset fasting requires aligning waking and mealtimes with the dawn and sunset of human creatures. Severe COVID-19 cases are associated with abnormalities in blood laboratory indicators (e.g., interleukin 6, C-reactive protein, lymphocytopenia, leukocytosis) and several comorbidities that impair the immune response (e.g., malignancy, diabetes, obesity). Several studies about dawn-to-sunset fasting are through inducing proteomic responses associated with reducing oxidative stress, increasing autophagy, suppressing inflammation, improving components of metabolic syndrome, and reshaping the gut microbiome. It was found that this fasting has the potential of optimizing immune system function against SARS-CoV-2, because it improves metabolic profiles, suppresses oxidative stress and chronic inflammation, and reshapes the gut microbiome [50].

Disruption of the viral cycle (protein synthesis) and the link that promotes autophagy may be a possible direct benefit of IF in COVID-19. In addition, the strong anti-inflammatory effects of IF may play a role in reducing the severity of COVID-19. Prospective randomized controlled clinical trials are needed in the future to evaluate IF regimens to prevent or treat moderate to severe COVID-19 in humans [51]. Some viral virulence factors can lyse cells to release nutrients, allowing bacteria to grow and cause secondary infections. Dietary regimens with IF may reduce the risk of secondary bacterial infections. Drugs that enhance autophagy help patients suppress secondary infections. When the situation becomes serious, the use of antibiotics or mixtures of antibiotics is necessary [52].

8. Immunity

IF can trigger multifaceted and comprehensive changes in energy metabolism, and these metabolic channels may fully interact with the immune system to trigger complex immune transformation. Ma explored how IF affects autophagy, oxidative stress, lipid metabolism, circadian rhythm, hormone levels, intestinal microbiota, and intestinal barrier integrity, and speculated on the mechanism of the interaction between the immune system and these factors [53].

Barati et al. reviewed studies on the role and impact of IF on autoimmune diseases, and the results showed that IF may have favorable effects on a variety of autoimmune diseases by regulating the immune system, reducing inflammatory markers, changing and improving the gut microbiota, and enhancing cell repair mechanisms. However, autophagy evidence for the effects of IF on autoimmune diseases is inconclusive and limited. However, IF may be a promising dietary intervention for the treatment of autoimmune diseases [54].

It has been shown that IF and caloric restriction improve autoimmune disease symptoms in animal models and patients, and also increase autophagy in plasma cells. Although systemic lupus erythematosus is an autoimmune disease, results show that IF worsens lupus nephritis in mice by increasing the formation of autoantibody immune complexes [55].

9. Cancers

Autophagy disorders can lead to many diseases such as cancers, and autophagy can play a role in promoting or inhibiting tumors, which is related to the tumor types. Cancer therapy regulated by autophagy is a treatment method that is being studied. Nutritional restriction such as fasting is a promising option for adjuvant cancer treatment, while achieving the anti-cancer effect of autophagy regulation and protecting normal cells [56]. Psara et al. summarized the application of existing clinical studies to study the effectiveness of IF on cancer progression and induction indicators.

The results show that the inhibition of various cancers seems to be achieved by IF through the induction of autophagy [57].

Autophagy induced by IF is achieved by activating a variety of biological pathways, which can promote cell renewal to prevent the proliferation of cancer cells and delay aging. However, IF has limitations and specific adverse effects when it comes to people of specific ages and genders, and more systematic studies are needed on the safety and health-promoting effects of IF [58].

10. Rhythms

Autophagy activation is stimulated by fasting states and is essential for cell function and integrity, with overnight fasting periods assisting in the maintenance of circadian rhythms [9]. Other studies have found that IF can regulate the circadian rhythm of hormones (such as leptin or insulin, etc.), and these hormone levels will change with food scarcity and abundance conditions [59].

11. Conclusions

Today, humans typically consume excessive amounts of food (at least tripling) per day, often leading to metabolic disease, and people can perform high levels of physiological and cognitive function during food fasting/deprivation [2]. A growing body of research shows that IF is a cleansing activity in terms of health and is an effective means of activating autophagy. After more than 16 hours of fasting, the triggered autophagy continues to have an impact on all tissues and organ systems when cellular-level regeneration is initiated. IF is a non-pharmacological dietary pattern that has several health-promoting effects, including prolonging life, assisting with drugs to fight tumors, improving neurological disorders, and reducing weight, fasting insulin levels, and blood sugar levels. IF prevents some of the adverse effects of chronic calorie restriction, such as malnutrition. Fasting or intermittent calorie restriction has many potential psychological and physical benefits [60]. Caloric restriction triggers a complex series of events, including activating elements of the cellular stress response, improving autophagy, regulating apoptosis, and altering hormonal balance.

Obesity and obesity-related diseases are largely the result of urbanization and lifestyle changes and are a global public health problem. Recently, as a dietary approach to managing obesity and metabolic syndrome, IF has been popular in mainstream culture. It has been shown to reduce body weight, reduce inflammation, and improve gut microbiome in humans. Teker et al. studied to determine the effects of 18-hour IF for 5 weeks on intestinal microbiota in rats, and found that IF resulted in significant bacterial diversity [61]. IF has multiple beneficial effects on most age-related degenerative changes in the body, such as prevention of age-related changes in the prostate, by improving autophagy, inhibiting oxidative stress, and anti-inflammatory and anti-proliferative effects. Because IF is safe and more readily available than therapeutic drugs, it has the potential for use in the treatment of benign prostatic hyperplasia [62]. IF and caloric restriction delay aging and extend life span in many species, and prevention of metabolic and age-related diseases can be achieved, for example, by lowering blood pressure and improving insulin sensitivity and inflammation. With the advent of a global aging world, the proportion of people over 60 years of age will increase significantly in 2050 in almost every region on Earth (except Antarctica). Potential interventions, including dietary restrictions, exercise, and plant foods, are safe and effective ways to regulate circadian rhythms and restore the imbalance of the aging body. Although autophagy in the aging process still has many unresolved problems, such as time and space regulation, as well as the autophagy threshold related to disease and benefits, it is more clear that balanced autophagy can maintain body health, in line with the traditional Chinese philosophy of Yin and Yang.

Although numerous studies have shown improvements associated with IF across a wide range of health conditions (such as aging, obesity, diabetes, cardiovascular disease, tumors, neurological and psychological disorders, stress, and immune system disorders), there are several challenges in this area. A smaller percentage of people are able to maintain intensive IF in reality [40]. The ratio of benefits to harms of IF varies with regimen, starting age and duration, and model [16]. There are a variety of research protocols, and the interpretation of weight loss trend is quite different. Most of the research results involving weight loss and metabolic biomarker improvement are different [16]. What often hinders the transfer of valid preclinical results in animal models to clinical applications of IF regimens are psychological and neurological disorders. Patients experience some transient calorie restriction side effects (e.g., hunger, reduced focus, irritability) that make adherence to the regimen impossible. In practice, only a very small number of people, including obese people, can practice calorie restriction for a long time. Therefore, it is necessary to develop food or drugs that mimic the effect of calorie restriction. The existing calorie restriction mimics include resveratrol, curcumin, aspirin, and metformin, etc., which cause autophagy, neutralize free radicals, change the expression of pro-apoptotic and anti-apoptotic factors, prevent protein aggregation, and chelate REDOX active metal ions. More valuable simulated calorie restriction options in the future could include vegetarian diets, Mediterranean diets, or local seasonal diets across China or around the world. In addition, potential problems during long-term calorie restriction include slowed metabolism, fatigue, nutritional deficiencies, decreased fertility, weak bones, and reduced immunity. The Chinese medical classic "Huangdi Neijing" recorded that "five kinds of grains are nourishing," so people's long-term food intake is insufficient, especially grain intake is insufficient, resulting in a series of problems. There are some opposite effects of IF on sleep. Several clinical studies have found that IF can improve mood in the short term, but further long-term clinical studies are needed to assess the duration of continuous improvement [13].

In conclusion, IF has a systematic effect on health improvement and is worth popularizing and applying widely in the future. However, there are many challenges. And long-term systematic studies are still needed in the future. We look forward to formulating standards for IF as soon as possible, including the precise optimal individual fasting regimen and applicable contraindications.

Conflict of interest

The authors declare no conflict of interest.

Author details

Ying Yang[1,2]

1 State Key Laboratory for Diagnosis and Treatment of Infectious Diseases, The First Affiliated Hospital, College of Medicine, Zhejiang University, Hangzhou, China

2 National Clinical Research Center for Infectious Diseases, The First Affiliated Hospital, College of Medicine, Zhejiang University, Hangzhou, China

*Address all correspondence to: zjuyangying@zju.edu.cn

References

[1] Mani K, Javaheri A, Diwan A. Lysosomes mediate benefits of intermittent fasting in cardiometabolic disease: The janitor is the undercover boss. Comprehensive Physiology. 2018;**8**(4):1639-1667. DOI: 10.1002/cphy.c180005

[2] Mattson MP, Longo VD, Harvie M. Impact of intermittent fasting on health and disease processes. Ageing Research Reviews. 2017;**39**:46-58. DOI: 10.1016/j.arr.2016.10.005

[3] Annalisa M. VanHook. Periodic dieting promotes health. Science Signaling. 2015;**8**(385):ec187. DOI: 10.1126/scisignal.aac9913

[4] Yang M, Chen W, He L, Liu D, Zhao L, Wang X. Intermittent fasting—A healthy dietary pattern for diabetic nephropathy. Nutrients. 2022;**14**(19):3995. DOI: 10.3390/nu14193995

[5] Michalsen A, Chenying LC. Fasting therapy for treating and preventing disease—Current state of evidence. Forschende Komplementärmedizin. 2013;**20**(6):444-453. DOI: 10.1159/000357765

[6] Ma YN, Jiang X, Tang W, Song P. Influence of intermittent fasting on autophagy in the liver. Bioscience Trends. 2023;**17**(5):335-355. DOI: 10.5582/bst.2023.01207

[7] Shabkhizan R, Haiaty S, Moslehian MS, et al. The beneficial and adverse effects of autophagic response to caloric restriction and fasting. Advances in Nutrition. 2023;**14**(5):1211-1225. DOI: 10.1016/j.advnut.2023.07.006

[8] Stratton MT, Albracht-Schulte K, Harty PS, et al. Physiological responses to acute fasting: Implications for intermittent fasting programs. Nutrition Reviews. 2022;**80**(3):439-452. DOI: 10.1093/nutrit/nuab094

[9] Veldscholte K, Cramer ABG, Joosten KFM, et al. Intermittent fasting in paediatric critical illness: The properties and potential beneficial effects of an overnight fast in the PICU. Clinical Nutrition. 2021;**40**(9):5122-5132. DOI: 10.1016/j.clnu.2021.07.030

[10] Jamshed H, Beyl RA, Della Manna DL, et al. Early time-restricted feeding improves 24-hour glucose levels and affects markers of the circadian clock, aging, and autophagy in humans. Nutrients. 2019;**11**(6):1234. DOI: 10.3390/nu11061234

[11] Minciuna I, Gallage S, Heikenwalder M, et al. Intermittent fasting-the future treatment in NASH patients? Hepatology. 2023;**78**(4):1290-1305. DOI: 10.1097/HEP.0000000000000330

[12] Lavallee CM, Bruno A, Ma C, et al. The role of intermittent fasting in the management of nonalcoholic fatty liver disease: A narrative review. Nutrients. 2022;**14**(21):4655. DOI: 10.3390/nu14214655

[13] Igwe O, Sone M, Matveychuk D, Baker GB, Dursun SM. A review of effects of calorie restriction and fasting with potential relevance to depression. Progress in Neuro-Psychopharmacology & Biological Psychiatry. 2021;**111**:110206. DOI: 10.1016/j.pnpbp.2020.110206

[14] Ebrahim HA, El-Gamal R, Sherif RN. Intermittent fasting attenuates high-fat diet-induced cerebellar changes in rats: Involvement of TNF-α, autophagy,

and oxidative stress. Cells, Tissues, Organs. 2021;**210**(5-6):351-367. DOI: 10.1159/000519088

[15] Sharma A, Singh AK. Molecular mechanism of caloric restriction mimetics-mediated neuroprotection of age-related neurodegenerative diseases: An emerging therapeutic approach. Biogerontology. 2023;**24**(5):679-708. DOI: 10.1007/s10522-023-10045-y

[16] Stockman MC, Thomas D, Burke J, et al. Intermittent fasting: Is the wait worth the weight? Current Obesity Reports. 2018;7(2):172-185. DOI: 10.1007/s13679-018-0308-9

[17] Sudasinghe K, White Z, Rogers L, et al. Effects of intermittent fasting on brain tissue in male Fisher-344 rats. Physiology. 2023;**38**(S1):1-3. DOI: 10.1152/physiol.2023.38.s1.5733650

[18] Ratliff EP, Kotzebue RW, Molina B, et al. Assessing basal and acute autophagic responses in the adult drosophila nervous system: The impact of gender, genetics and diet on endogenous pathway profiles. PLoS ONE. 2016;**11**(10):e0164239. DOI: 10.1371/journal.pone.0164239

[19] Ntsapi CM, Loos B. Neurons die with heightened but functional macro- and chaperone mediated autophagy upon increased amyloid-ß induced toxicity with region-specific protection in prolonged intermittent fasting. Experimental Cell Research. 2021;**408**(2):112840. DOI: 10.1016/j.yexcr.2021.112840

[20] Wells RG, Neilson LE, McHill AW, et al. Dietary fasting and time-restricted eating in Huntington's disease: Therapeutic potential and underlying mechanisms. Translational Neurodegeneration. 2024;**13**(1):17. DOI: 10.1186/s40035-024-00406-z

[21] Ehrnhoefer DE, Martin DDO, Schmidt ME, et al. Preventing mutant huntingtin proteolysis and intermittent fasting promote autophagy in models of Huntington disease. Acta Neuropathologica Communications. 2018;**6**(1):16. DOI: 10.1186/s40478-018-0518-0

[22] Xu Y, Liu Z, Xu S, et al. Scientific evidences of calorie restriction and intermittent fasting for neuroprotection in traumatic brain injury animal models: A review of the literature. Nutrients. 2022;**14**(7):1431. DOI: 10.3390/nu14071431

[23] Jeong JH, Yu KS, Bak DH, et al. Intermittent fasting is neuroprotective in focal cerebral ischemia by minimizing autophagic flux disturbance and inhibiting apoptosis. Experimental and Therapeutic Medicine. 2016;**12**(5):3021-3028. DOI: 10.3892/etm.2016.3852

[24] Yuan W, He X, Morin D, et al. Autophagy induction contributes to the neuroprotective impact of intermittent fasting on the acutely injured spinal cord. Journal of Neurotrauma. 2021;**38**(3):373-384. DOI: 10.1089/neu.2020.7166

[25] Agaty SME, Nassef NA, Abou-bakr DA, et al. The effect of intermittent fasting on isoproterenol-induced myocardial infarction in aged rats: A potential role of autophagy. QJM: An International Journal of Medicine. 2023;**116**(Suppl.1):1. DOI: 10.1093/qjmed/hcad069.686

[26] Forte M, Rodolico D, Ameri P, et al. Molecular mechanisms underlying the beneficial effects of exercise and dietary interventions in the prevention of cardiometabolic diseases. Journal of Cardiovascular Medicine (Hagerstown, Md.). 2023;**24**(Suppl. 1):e3-e14. DOI: 10.2459/JCM.0000000000001397

[27] El Agaty SM, Nassef NA, Abou-Bakr DA, et al. Chronic activation of cardiac Atg-5 and pancreatic Atg-7 by intermittent fasting alleviates acute myocardial infarction in old rats. The Egyptian Heart Journal. 2022;**74**(1):31. DOI: 10.1186/s43044-022-00268-8

[28] Godar RJ, Ma X, Liu H, et al. Repetitive stimulation of autophagy-lysosome machinery by intermittent fasting preconditions the myocardium to ischemia-reperfusion injury. Autophagy. 2015;**11**(9):1537-1560. DOI: 10.1080/15548627.2015.1063768

[29] Ozcan M, Guo Z, Ripoll CV, et al. Intermittent fasting potentiates anthracycline cardiotoxicity. Journal of Cardiac Failure. 2023;**29**(4):568. DOI: 10.1016/j.cardfail.2022.10.057

[30] Abas E, Sabry M. Intermittent fasting attenuates apoptosis, modulates autophagy and preserve telocytes in doxorubicin induced cardiotoxicity in albino rats: A histological study Egyptian. Journal of Histology. 2020;**43**(3):663-682. DOI: 10.21608/ejh.2020.22181.1230

[31] Chaudhary R, Liu B, Bensalem J, et al. Intermittent fasting activates markers of autophagy in mouse liver, but not muscle from mouse or humans. Nutrition. 2022;**101**:111662. DOI: 10.1016/j.nut.2022.111662

[32] Semenovich DS, Zorova LD, Abramicheva PA, et al. Impact of intermittent fasting and dietary restriction on Redox state, energetic metabolism, and liver injury in common bile duct ligation model. Antioxidants (Basel). 2024;**13**(7):835. DOI: 10.3390/antiox13070835

[33] Deng Q, Lv R, Zou H, et al. Beneficial effects of intermittent fasting on nonalcoholic fatty liver disease: A narrative review. Egyptian Liver Journal. 2024;**14**(63):1-15. DOI: 10.1186/s43066-024-00368-x

[34] Hosny SA, Moustafa MHA, Mehina FM, et al. Therapeutic effect of autophagy induced by rapamycin versus intermittent fasting in animal model of fatty liver. Folia Histochemica et Cytobiologica. 2023;**61**(4):205-216. DOI: 10.5603/fhc.95905

[35] Gong PF, Jiang ZR, Huang X, et al. Long-term intermittent fasting induces abnormal lipid accumulation in mouse liver. Sheng Li Xue Bao. 2022;**74**(6):962-969

[36] Li D, Dun Y, Qi D, et al. Intermittent fasting activates macrophage migration inhibitory factor and alleviates high-fat diet-induced nonalcoholic fatty liver disease. Scientific Reports. 2023;**13**(1):13068. DOI: 10.1038/s41598-023-40373-5

[37] Liu T, Liu Y, Yan T, et al. Intermittent fasting, exercise, and dietary modification induce unique transcriptomic signatures of multiple tissues governing metabolic homeostasis during weight loss and rebound weight gain. The Journal of Nutritional Biochemistry. 2024;**130**:109649. DOI: 10.1016/j.jnutbio.2024.109649

[38] Wang Z, Yu L, Fu Y. Comparison of intermittent fasting and exercise on skeletal muscle autophagy activation and fat reduction. Zhongguo Ying Yong Sheng Li Xue Za Zhi. 2020;**36**(4):289-295. DOI: 10.12047/j.cjap.5942.2020.063

[39] Yoshii R, Higashida K, Nakai N. Intermittent fasting reduces mouse body fat while maintaining muscle mass by regulating protein synthesis and autophagy. Nutrition. 2023;**115**:112130. DOI: 10.1016/j.nut.2023.112130

[40] Zhang Y, Finck BN, DeBosch BJ. Driving arginine catabolism to activate systemic autophagy. Autophagy Reports. 2022;**1**(1):65-69. DOI: 10.1080/27694127.2022.2040763

[41] Chen L, Tian FY, Hu XH, et al. Intermittent fasting in type 2 diabetes: From fundamental science to clinical applications. European Review for Medical and Pharmacological Sciences. 2023;**27**(1):333-351. DOI: 10.26355/eurrev_202301_30880

[42] Hassan NH, Saleh D, El-Khair SMA, et al. The relation between autophagy modulation by intermittent fasting and aquaporin 2 expression in experimentally induced diabetic nephropathy in albino rat. Tissue & Cell. 2024;**88**:102395. DOI: 10.1016/j.tice.2024.102395

[43] Taha RI, Alghamdi MA, Alshehri H, et al. Streptozotocin- induced changes in aquaporin 1 and 4, oxidative stress, and autophagy in submandibular and parotid salivary glands and the possible ameliorative effect of intermittent fasting on these changes. Tissue and Cell. 2023;**85**:102242. DOI: 10.1016/j.tice.2023.102242

[44] Castelblanco E, Shyr ZA, Yan Z, et al. 318-OR: Intermittent fasting improves ß-cell function in nonobese KATP-induced neonatal diabetes through reduction of cellular stress and enhanced autophagy. Diabetes. 2022. DOI: 10.2337/db22-318-or

[45] Hafez SMNA, Elbassuoni E. Dysfunction of aged liver of male albino rats and the effect of intermitted fasting; Biochemical, histological, and immunohistochemical study. International Immunopharmacology. 2022;**103**:108465. DOI: 10.1016/j.intimp.2021.108465

[46] Abokyi S, Kwansah GG, Tse DYY. TFEB is a central regulator of the aging process and age-related diseases. Ageing Research Reviews. 2023;**89**:101985. DOI: 10.1016/j.arr.2023.101985

[47] Wong S, Cabo RD, Bernier M, et al. Metabolic flexibility: Interplay of diet composition and intermittent fasting on healthspan (P08-053-19). Current Developments in Nutrition. 2019;**3**(Suppl.1):2120. DOI: 10.1093/cdn/nzz044.p08-053-19

[48] Saini SK, Singh A, Saini M, et al. Time-restricted eating regimen differentially affects circulatory miRNA expression in older overweight adults. Nutrients. 2022;**14**(9):1843. DOI: 10.3390/nu14091843

[49] Hannan MA, Rahman MA, Rahman MS, et al. Intermittent fasting, a possible priming tool for host defense against SARS-CoV-2 infection: Crosstalk among calorie restriction, autophagy and immune response. Immunology Letters. 2020;**226**:38-45. DOI: 10.1016/j.imlet.2020.07.001

[50] Bhatti SI, Mindikoglu AL. The impact of dawn to sunset fasting on immune system and its clinical significance in COVID-19 pandemic. Metabolism Open. 2022;**13**:100162. DOI: 10.1016/j.metop.2021.100162

[51] Gnoni M, Beas R, Vásquez-Garagatti R. Is there any role of intermittent fasting in the prevention and improving clinical outcomes of COVID-19?: Intersection between inflammation, mTOR pathway, autophagy and calorie restriction. Virus. 2021;**32**(4):625-634. DOI: 10.1007/s13337-021-00703-5

[52] Zhang Y, An S, Ye ZW, et al. How to prevent secondary infections by bacteria in heart disease patients. European Journal of Preventive

Cardiology. 2018;**25**(13):1433. DOI: 10.1177/2047487318778642

[53] Ma RX. A detective story of intermittent fasting effect on immunity. Immunology. 2024;**173**:227-247. DOI: 10.1111/imm.13829

[54] Barati M, Ghahremani A, Ahmadabad HN. Intermittent fasting: A promising dietary intervention for autoimmune diseases. Autoimmunity Reviews. 2023;**22**(10):103408. DOI: 10.1016/j.autrev.2023.103408

[55] Hong SM, Lee J, Jang SG, et al. Intermittent fasting aggravates lupus nephritis through increasing survival and autophagy of antibody secreting cells in MRL/lpr mice. International Journal of Molecular Sciences. 2020;**21**(22):8477. DOI: 10.3390/ijms21228477

[56] Antunes F, Erustes AG, Costa AJ, et al. Autophagy and intermittent fasting: The connection for cancer therapy? Clinics (São Paulo, Brazil). 2018;**73**(suppl. 1):e814s. DOI: 10.6061/clinics/2018/e814s

[57] Psara E, Poulios E, Papadopoulou SK, et al. Intermittent fasting against cancer development and progression: Highlighting potential anticancer molecular mechanisms. Anti-Cancer Agents in Medicinal Chemistry. 2023;**23**(17):1889-1909. DOI: 10.2174/1871520623666230816090229

[58] Liu S, Zeng M, Wan W, et al. The health-promoting effects and the mechanism of intermittent fasting. Journal Diabetes Research. 2023;**2023**:4038546. DOI: 10.1155/2023/4038546

[59] Joaquim L, Faria A, Loureiro H, et al. Benefits, mechanisms, and risks of intermittent fasting in metabolic syndrome and type 2 diabetes. Journal of Physiology and Biochemistry. 2022;**78**(2):295-305. DOI: 10.1007/s13105-021-00839-4

[60] Golbidi S, Daiber A, Korac B, Li H, et al. Health benefits of fasting and caloric restriction. Current Diabetes Reports. 2017;**17**(12):123. DOI: 10.1007/s11892-017-0951-7

[61] Teker HT, Ceylani T. Intermittent fasting supports the balance of the gut microbiota composition. International Microbiology. 2023;**26**(1):51-57. DOI: 10.1007/s10123-022-00272-7

[62] Gamal El-Tahawy NF, Rifaai RA. Intermittent fasting protects against age-induced rat benign prostatic hyperplasia via preservation of prostatic histomorphology, modification of oxidative stress, and beclin-1/P62 pathway. Microscopy and Microanalysis. 2023;**29**(3):1267-1276. DOI: 10.1093/micmic/ozad035

Chapter 6

The Interplay of Pathology, Prevention and Treatment in Cardio-Metabolic Diseases

Sana Qausain, Mohd Basheeruddin and Ashish Anjankar

Abstract

This chapter explores the intricate relationship between heart disorders and metabolism disorders, sometimes known as cardio-metabolic diseases. These illnesses, hypertension, diabetes, metabolic syndrome, and coronary artery disease, have similar underlying pathophysiological mechanisms and risk factors. This chapter explores the epidemiology of cardio-metabolic disorders, emphasising the significant global health burden associated with these conditions as well as their rising prevalence. Insulin resistance, dyslipidemia, endothelial dysfunction, and chronic inflammation are some critical pathophysiological pathways highlighted. Cardio-metabolic diseases are linked and proceed through these processes. The genesis and management of various disorders are also examined in this chapter in light of genetic, environmental, and lifestyle variables. The risk of cardio-metabolic disorders is decreased, and preventive interventions, such as dietary and physical activity changes and weight management, manage their progression. The chapter also analyses new medicines and current pharmaceutical treatments to enhance therapeutic results and target the underlying mechanisms. New insights into potential future routes for prevention and therapy are provided by emerging research on the role of the gut microbiome, innovative biomarkers, and personalised medicine techniques. In order to enhance patient outcomes and lessen the associated healthcare burden, the chapter's conclusion emphasises the significance of a multidisciplinary approach in the treatment of cardio-metabolic illnesses.

Keywords: cardiovascular disease, cardio-metabolic diseases, metabolic syndrome, chronic inflammation, dyslipidemia and gut microbiome

1. Introduction

Cardio-metabolic diseases entail CVD, T2DM, and MetS as part of its continuum of diseases that occur due to metabolic dysfunction. These conditions are closely interrelated with other symptoms of pathophysiological mechanisms and risk factors, which include obesity, hypertension, dyslipidemia and insulin resistance. Familiarity with such relations is critical for identifying appropriate prevention and treatment measures for these diseases [1].

The main objective of this chapter is to acquaint the reader with the basic facts on the developments of cardio-metabolic syndrome and its risk factors, preventive measures and potential treatment options. We will also describe future developments in treatments and ongoing development and research with the potential to enhance patient care.

1.1 Cardiovascular disease (CVD)

This includes diseases of the cardiovascular system such as coronary artery disease, heart failure and stroke. CVD continues to be reported as the number one cause of death in the world [2].

1.2 Type 2 diabetes mellitus (T2DM)

T2DM is further characterised by insulin resistance and poor first-phase insulin secretion resulting in maintained hyperglycemia and chronicity, T2DM, [3] is complex and has hazardous complications such as cardiovascular disease, neuropathies, nephropathies and retinopathies.

1.3 Metabolic syndrome

This is a group of metabolic disturbances that are associated with obesity, particularly central obesity, high serum triglycerides, low HDL cholesterol, high blood pressure and high fasting blood glucose, which all lead to increased susceptibility to cardiovascular diseases and non-insulin-dependent diabetes [4].

1.4 Traditional treatments

The primary treatment of cardio-metabolic diseases generally requires adherence to a line of treatment that is characterised by the use of various interventions such as alteration of behaviours and the use of drugs that can help reduce the various risk factors to a certain extent to minimise complications.

1.4.1 Lifestyle modifications

The principles of dietary modification entail using fruits and vegetables, whole grain products, lean meats, low-fat dairy products, and healthy fats to prevent and control cardio-metabolic diseases. One can emphasise the concrete examples of the scope, including the so-called Mediterranean diet, which has been proven to positively impact CV risk and metabolic profiles [5]. Aero-villain and resistance exercises should be implemented in the daily routine since they strengthen the cardiac muscle, increase insulin sensitivity, and even help shed pounds [6]. The models also increase patients' awareness of the health benefits of reaching and sustaining a healthy weight, which will help prevent diabetes and cardiovascular diseases. Lifestyle changes involve weight loss, which is a common intervention utilised for overweight and obese clients.

Total abstinence from tobacco has the effect of lessening the incidence of cardiovascular episodes and enhancing health. Of all the measures that can be taken in order to prevent cardiovascular disease, the one to stop smoking undoubtedly ranks high. Also, avoiding or taking a moderate amount of alcohol helps regulate the pressure level and prevent liver and cardiovascular illnesses [7]. The health effects of alcohol are said to be wrong, hence the call for people to limit their consumption of alcohol. Altogether, these changes are invaluable when it comes to the prevention and control of cardio-metabolic diseases.

1.4.2 Pharmacological interventions

Cardio-metabolic diseases mostly require medication to address the problem or ease the symptoms. ACE inhibitors, ARBs, beta-blockers, calcium channel blockers and diuretics are antihypertensives that decrease blood pressure and cardiovascular risk [8]. Statin, fibrates and PCSK9 inhibitors are used in the management of dyslipidemia and prevention of ASCVD. Thus, for patients with T2DM, the pharmacological management of glycemia utilises medications like metformin, sulfonylureas, DPP-4 inhibitors, GLP-1 receptor agonists and SGLT2 inhibitors [9]. Further, aspirin and other antiplatelet drugs are used to prevent thrombotic processes in cardiovascular disease patients.

1.5 Need for complementary approaches

Conventional therapies are helpful in cardio-metabolic diseases; therefore, there is a rising interest in refinement manners that may help these patients tackle these intricate illnesses.

1.5.1 Integrative medicine

The existing researches prove the effectiveness of specific dietary supplements, including Omega-3 fatty acids, Antioxidants, and Plant sterols and their contribution to improving cardiovascular and metabolic health [10]. Besides, activities such as mindfulness, yoga and meditation also help reduce stress, thus reducing glycemic index and an individual's general cardiovascular health. Acupuncture therapy, Ayurveda therapy and other traditional medical therapies, the theories mentioned above, manage cardio-metabolic diseases physically and mentally through fit and delicate balance.

1.5.2 Personalised medicine

With modern knowledge of genomics and proteomics, each patient's prognosis and risk factors can be determined, and an appropriate treatment plan can be planned without compromising the patient [11]. The role of biomarkers in interventions that target and optimise both effectiveness rates and negative consequences of therapy would positively impact patients. Individualised diets derived from an individual's genetic makeup, metabolism, and gut microbiome could enhance traditional dietary interventions and, therefore, can play a role in controlling cardio-metabolic diseases.

The approach used in cardio-metabolic diseases is multidimensional because these diseases' pathology, prevention, and treatment are complex. Suppose conventional and CAM, as well as patient-tailored methods, are used jointly to treat these diseases. In that case, healthcare providers can help patients and alleviate the impact of such diseases and chronic conditions in the long run. Therefore, further investigation and developments are required for better effective prevention and treatment strategies of cardio-metabolic diseases in the changing perspective of health care [12].

2. Historical overview of treatment in cardio-metabolic diseases

The management of cardio-metabolic diseases has undergone milestones of changes in the twentieth century through medical achievement, technological enhancement and increased health consciousness about disease aetiology. This historic literature review aims to identify significant events in cardiology history and the steady improvement of the methods used to treat cardiovascular diseases, T2DM, and metabolic syndrome.

2.1 Early twentieth century: Emergence of modern medicine

Cardiovascular diseases and diabetes at the beginning of the twentieth century were not nearly as well managed as they are now; the management included dieting primarily and exercise. Frederick Banting and Charles Best discovered insulin in 1921, which was a very significant discovery for patients with diabetes, mainly type 1 diabetes, but later beneficial for T2DM patients as well [13]. At the same time, the knowledge of cardiovascular disease (CVD) as a medical concept was evolving, and practitioners' early attempts to address CVD involved the treatment of symptoms and perhaps surgical operations for severe cases [14].

2.2 Mid-twentieth century: Pharmacological breakthroughs

The middle of the twentieth century can be characterised as a breakthrough in pharmacology in treating cardio-metabolic illnesses. The discovery of oral hypoglycaemic agents for T2DM consisted of larger classes that preceded the 1950s sulphonylureas. In the cardiovascular disease world, antihypertensive drugs such as thiazide diuretics, beta-blockers and calcium channel blockers heralded changed ways of preventing and managing hypertension-related complications [15].

2.3 1970s–1980s: Lipid management and lifestyle interventions

This knowledge was significantly delimited in the course of the 1970s and early 1980s when lipids and their place in cardiovascular diseases gained essential acknowledgement. Statins came into use in 1987 when lovastatin was approved and completely changed the paradigm of lipid treatment and the resulting prevalence of atherosclerotic cardiovascular disease. This period was characterised by introducing the concept of lifestyle changes including diet, exercise, and smoking as critical factors in cardio-metabolic diseases [16].

2.4 1990s–2000s: Integrative approaches and evidence-based medicine

The two decades of the nineties and two thousand meant the integration into cardio-metabolic diseases of evidence-based medicine. Essential studies offered solid references for the clinical application of more extensive forms of specific therapeutic methods. New oral antidiabetic drugs, including metformin, thiazolidinediones, and more recently, DPP-IV inhibitors and GLP-1 receptor agonists, enriched the armoury in managing T2DM [17]. At the same time, betterments occurred in the stakes of invasive procedures such as CABG and PCI, as well as additional efficacious treatments for patients with severe cardiovascular disorders [18].

2.5 2010s-present: Personalised medicine and novel therapies

The last 10 years have brought positive changes in using genomic and proteomic patterns to increase a patient's treatment outcome. Biomarkers have been adopted in the administration of therapies with a definite impact on the precision of the interventions [19]. Modern drugs include PCSK9 inhibitors for lipid control and SGLT2 inhibitors for T2DM, which have yielded tremendous results in decreasing CVD risk. Also, supplemental and holistic methods such as nutraceuticals, mind-body interventions, and traditional medicine have received a positive reception as adjuvant therapy for cardio-metabolic diseases [20].

In managing cardio-metabolic diseases, the initial management was dietary and lifestyle changes, while pharmacological and surgical management are used in the current world. The continuous development of the specific approaches to care and the ways of combining long-term conventional contra- and co-treatments indicate the avenues for further improving the general management and outcomes of these multifactorial diseases. New knowledge in the understanding of cardio-metabolic diseases is identified, and the development of any molecular, gene, cellular, or other targeted therapies still in the experimental stage or even at the drawing board today is predicated on the belief that practical specific approaches to control cardio-metabolic diseases and its manifestations will be the treatment of tomorrow [21].

3. Pathophysiology

The mechanisms of development of cardio-metabolic diseases are based on the principles of genetics, life experience, and social environment. These include insulin stearness, chronic inflammation, dyslipidemia, and hypertension. These processes are closely related and impact the creation and advancement of metabolic and cardiovascular diseases [22].

3.1 Insulin resistance and hyperinsulinemia

T2DM and MetS are characterised by insulin resistance as one of their significant features. It happens when cells in the body start to decrease their ability to process insulin, and therefore, high blood glucose levels are experienced. As a response, the pancreas releases more insulin and has a hyperinsulinemia condition among the affected population. Hyperinsulinemia and insulin resistance lead to atherogenic, hypertension, and dyslipidemia, which are some of the causes of CVD [23].

3.2 Chronic inflammation

Low-grade inflammation is observed in cardio-metabolic diseases and is considered to be chronic. TNF-alpha and IL-6 pro-inflammatory cytokines raised in obesity, T2DM, and MetS. These cytokines contribute to the worsening of insulin signalling and endothelial perturbation and, thus, atherosclerosis and cardiovascular disease [24].

3.3 Dyslipidemia

It is a condition in which triglyceride levels are high while High-Density Lipoprotein Cholesterol (HDL-C) levels are low, and Low-Density Lipoprotein Cholesterol (LDL-C) levels are high. These lipid abnormalities play a role in the development of atherosclerosis, which in turn leads to coronary artery disease and stroke [25].

3.4 Hypertension

Hypertension or high blood pressure is another complication frequently associated with T2DM and MetS. It is promoted by insulin resistance, dyslipidemia and endothelial disorder. Hypertension increases the severity of cardiovascular events such as heart attack and stroke to the next level [26].

4. Risk factors

Cardio-metabolic diseases depend on changing and unchangeable risk factors.

4.1 Modifiable risk factors

Population using SDFA, sugars, processed foods and excessive calories will likely develop obesity, T2DM and CVD. Physical inactivity also plays a vital role in these diseases since those people who are physically inactive put on weight and develop insulin resistance and dyslipidemia. Thus, the consumption of unhealthy food and the sedentary lifestyle feed each other and substantially increase the threat of cardio-metabolic diseases. Abdominal obesity is, therefore, a critical determinant of the onset of metabolic disease states, including insulin resistance, T2DM and CVD. These risks are further increased by smoking due to the effects it has on the blood vessels, inflammation, as well as atherogenesis [27]. Likewise, binge drinking with alcohol provokes hypertension, dyslipidemia, and obesity, as depicted in **Figure 1**, thus associating with the cardio-metabolic burden. It is worth underlining that changes in the mentioned factors are crucial for preventing and controlling these diseases [28].

4.2 Non-modifiable risk factors

A family history of cardio-metabolic disease is strongly associated with the expression and onset of cardio-metabolic diseases such as CVD and T2DM. Further, these

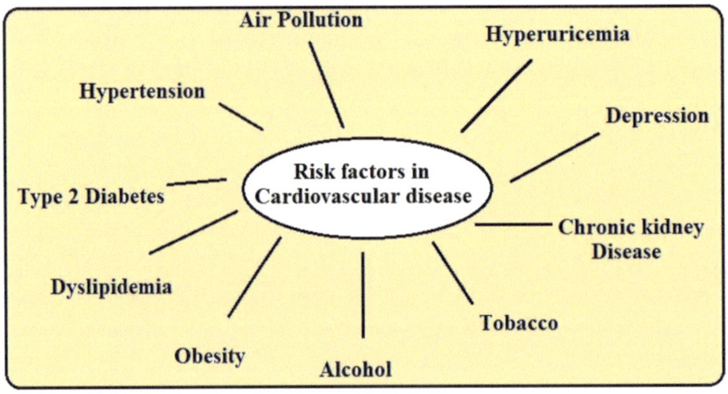

Figure 1.
Highlights the multifaceted nature of risk factors.

diseases tend to be more frequent in patients of advanced age. Sex also counts, and it is obvious that men are more susceptible to CVD than women. However, the latter see their risk rise immediately after menopause because of fluctuations in oestrogen levels [29].

5. Prevention strategies

Preventing cardio-metabolic diseases is thus a combined process that focuses on altering lifestyles as well as clinical management.

5.1 Lifestyle modifications

The intake of a Mediterranean diet that contains high eligibility of fruits, vegetables, whole grain products, fish, white meat, nuts and sources of monosaturated fatty acids reduces the risk factors of obesity, dyslipidemia and hypertension to a great extent. This focuses on healthy foods for cardiovascular and metabolic health status. Exercise such as aerobic exercise such as walking, running, and cycling and resistance exercises moderate insulin resistance, enhance weight loss and lower blood pressure [30]. Regularity in the habits of exercising has been deemed critical in the management of cardiovascular fitness as well as weight.

The patients avoided an average body size, diet and exercise that helps reduce insulin resistance, T2DM and CVD. Also, smoking cessation is recommended in order to avoid the development of atherosclerosis, hypertension and other complications of cardiovascular aetiology. Reducing alcohol consumption to a moderate level of a tiny drink per day for women and up to two small drinks for men reduces hypertension and dyslipidemia, which, in turn, reinforces heart health [31].

5.2 Pharmacological interventions

Medications used in the management of hypertension include ACE inhibitors, ARBs, Beta-blockers, and diuretics. In managing glucose levels, type 2 diabetes mellitus (T2DM) patients use antidiabetic agents such as metformin, sulfonylureas, thiazolidinediones and GLP-1 receptor agonists. Also, one can discover novel therapies for targeting inflammation, including monoclonal antibodies against pro-inflammatory cytokines, possibly reducing cardiovascular risk through managing the inflammatory component of cardio-metabolic diseases [32].

6. Treatment approaches

Cardio-metabolic diseases are managed through lifestyle modifications and the administration of medication. The management depends on the patient's needs (**Table 1**) [33].

6.1 Non-pharmacological interventions

Diet, physical activity, and weight are still essential components of treating cardio-metabolic diseases, even in the conditions of population ageing. Psycho-social therapy that involves counselling and encouragement for smoking cessation and moderate alcohol intake are also components of comprehensive disorders that assist the

Treatment approaches		
Non-pharmacological interventions	• Diet • Physical activity • Weight management • Psycho-social therapy (smoking cessation and moderate alcohol intake)	
Pharmacological treatments	Combination therapy	• Statins • Antihypertensive therapy • Antidiabetic medications
	New therapeutics	SGLT2 inhibitors for heart failure
Surgical interventions	Bariatric surgery	• Substantial weight loss • Improved metabolic profile
	Cardiovascular procedures	• Angioplasty • Coronary Artery Bypass Grafting (CABG), • To establish blood flow

Table 1.
Summarising the treatment approaches for cardio-metabolic diseases.

patient in changing habits that are compatible with the disease and enhance overall health and well-being in response to compliance to medical treatment [34].

6.2 Pharmacological treatments

6.2.1 Combination therapy

Taking one drug for separate characteristics of the disease and another for different characteristics, such as statins, jointly with antihypertensive therapy and antidiabetic medications [35].

6.2.2 New therapeutics

New molecules acting on specific pathophysiological processes, including SGLT2 inhibitors for T2DM and heart failure, are available [36].

6.3 Surgical interventions

6.3.1 Bariatric surgery

Thus, for patients with severe obesity, bariatric surgery can lead to substantial weight loss and beneficial changes in the metabolic profile and lower the risk of T2DM and CVD [37].

6.3.2 Cardiovascular procedures

Invasive procedures like angioplasty, coronary artery bypass grafting (CABG), etc., are employed to re-establish blood flow in patients with severe atherosclerosis and chronic ischaemic heart disease (CHD) [38].

7. Newer approaches to interventions and ideas for future study

Cardio-metabolic diseases are among the most dynamic health areas, with further research still being conducted about the new therapeutic approaches and interventions that may help enhance patients' prognosis.

7.1 Gene therapy

The gene therapy method is designed to influence such gene functions as insulin resistance, atherogenesis, and other aspects of cardio-metabolic syndromes. Thus, the disease process may be halted or reversed, provided the right genes are adjusted somehow [39].

7.2 Biological therapies

Biological modifiers of inflammation and lipid metabolism are in different stages of development as the next generation of therapeutic agents. For instance, drugs known as PCSK9 inhibitors have been revealed to be effective in reducing LDL-C and the occurrence of cardiovascular complications [40].

7.3 Precision medicine

Precision medicine, therefore, involves treating patients depending on their genetic makeup and other factors like the environment and day-to-day activities. Progress in genomics, proteomics and metabolomics allows the discovery of biomarkers to help manage patients according to their molecular profile [41].

8. Conclusion

Cardio-metabolic diseases are a major global threat as they affect the world's population and are characterised by multifactorial and intertwined pathological processes and high lethality. In this chapter, the author establishes an interconnected Web explaining how factors such as insulin resistance, chronic inflammation, dyslipidemia, and hypertension contribute to the progression of cardiovascular diseases, type 2 diabetes mellitus, and metabolic syndrome. It will, therefore, be easier to develop solutions to work on the interrelated processes, if any, over man's health and the resultant prevention and adequate management of these conditions.

8.1 Summary of findings

8.1.1 Pathophysiology

Pre-existing insulin resistance contributes to both metabolic as well as cardiovascular diseases, causing hyperinsulinemia, which fosters atherogenesis. Moderate systemic inflammation, characterised by elevated concentrations of inflammatory cytokines, promotes insulin resistance and atherogenic changes in the endothelium. A metabolic disorder marked by abnormal levels of lipids in the body causes atherosclerosis; therefore, there is an association with the risk of cardiovascular diseases. A patient with hypertension and corresponding metabolic disorders becomes even more vulnerable to cardiovascular incidents.

8.1.2 Risk factors

Primary behavioural and metabolic clusters, which can be altered easily, are diet, physical activity, obesity, smoking, and alcohol consumption are the key risk factors for cardio-metabolic diseases. Immutability characteristics that include genetics, age, and sex also play a role in determining one's vulnerability to the conditions.

8.1.3 Prevention strategies

Thus, there is a need for lifestyle changes such as consuming a healthy diet by avoiding bad cholesterol, exercising, maintaining your weight, avoiding smoking and avoiding excessive intake of alcohol. Therapeutic benefits of pharmacological attainment include statins, antihypertensive, antidiabetic medications and anti-inflammatory drugs.

8.1.4 Treatment approaches

Treatment is based on changes in lifestyles, medications, and surgery is also recommended in some cases. New directions through advanced technologies such as gene therapy, biological therapies, and precision medicine applications can be targeted at enhancing the patients' status.

8.2 Future directions

Cardio-metabolic disease will be managed based on the patient's genetic, environmental, and lifestyle characteristics in the future due to precision medicine. Key areas of focus for future research and development include: Key areas of focus for future research and development include:

8.2.1 Gene therapy

Further development of gene therapy for particular genes implicated in insulin signalling, lipid metabolism, etc., associated with cardio-metabolic risk.

8.2.2 Biological therapies

Create new biological drugs to address inflammation and lipid metabolism to a greater extent than approved drugs like monoclonal antibodies and other biologics are presently doing.

8.2.3 Precision medicine

Using omics data in genomics, proteomics, and metabolomics to determine prospect biomarkers and allow scientists to prescribe individual tailored therapy.

8.2.4 Integrated care models

Supporting integrated care approaches that include lifestyle modifications, pharmacological, and behavioural management of cardio-metabolic diseases.

8.2.5 Public health initiatives

Enhancing the approaches designed to implement the changes in the scale and distribution of health risks by using education, policy, and other community-available tools.

8.3 Closing remarks

Due to this fact, the concepts of pathology, prevention and treatment of cardiometabolic diseases are ideally balanced to show that the diseases are complex and should be tackled using numerous approaches. By making strides in knowledge of the causal factors and modifiable risk factors and progress in prevention and treatment interventions, we can substantially decrease the impact of these diseases on people and society. Thus, further studies, multilateral cooperation, and maintaining focus on patient-oriented approaches are crucial for enhancing the given and, therefore, the overall health of the population.

Acknowledgements

We are deeply grateful to everyone who helped us finish this chapter on fasting and its effects on the prevention and treatment of cancer.

We especially want to thank PhD supervisor, Dr. Khurshid A. Khan, BSA Crescent Institute of Science & Technology in Chennai, India. Their advice and experience in evaluating the scientific material have greatly improved this chapter's readability and significance with their Perceptive comments and recommendations. We want to express our gratitude to Dr. Abhay Gadhaine, Dean, and Dr. Archana Dhok, Head of the Department of Biochemistry at JNMC, DMIHER, Wardha, India, for allowing us to write this chapter on a crucial topic and providing a great platform and taking the time to discuss it.

We express our gratitude to Dr. Zaheeruddin Qazi Head of CRL, for his consistent assistance and encouragement, which made the research and writing of this chapter easier. His dedication to the progress of science has been essential in the search for new oncology therapy strategies.

Conflict of interest

The authors declare no conflicts of interest that could influence the impartiality of the content presented in this chapter.

Disclaimer

The information presented in this chapter is intended for educational purposes and should not substitute professional medical advice. Readers are encouraged to consult healthcare professionals regarding any medical concerns or decisions related to fasting and cancer treatment.

Ethical considerations

This chapter adheres to ethical guidelines regarding the reporting of research involving human subjects and animals. All studies referenced have been conducted with appropriate ethical approvals and consent.

Appendix A. Nomenclature

Atherosclerosis	The buildup of fats, cholesterol, and other substances in and on the artery walls.
Endothelial dysfunction	A type of non-obstructive coronary artery disease that causes inadequate blood supply.
Dyslipidemia	An abnormal amount of lipids in the blood.
Hyperinsulinemia	Excess levels of insulin circulating in the blood relative to the level of glucose.
Pro-inflammatory cytokines	Substances secreted by certain cells of the immune system that promote inflammation.

Appendix B. Abbreviations

CABG	coronary artery bypass grafting
CVD	cardiovascular disease
HDL-C	high-density lipoprotein cholesterol
IL-6	interleukin-6
LDL-C	low-density lipoprotein cholesterol
MetS	metabolic syndrome
TNF-α	tumour necrosis factor-alpha
T2DM	type 2 diabetes mellitus
ACE	angiotensin-converting enzyme
ARBs	angiotensin II receptor blockers
GLP-1	glucagon-like peptide-1
SGLT2	sodium-glucose co-transporter-2
PCSK9	proprotein convertase subtilisin/kexin type 9

DOI: http://dx.doi.org/10.5772/intechopen.1006567

Author details

Sana Qausain*, Mohd Basheeruddin and Ashish Anjankar
Department of Biochemistry, Jawaharlal Nehru Medical College, Datta Meghe Institute of Higher Education and Research, Wardha, India

*Address all correspondence to: binishsana@gmail.com

References

[1] Smith J, Brown K. Cardio-metabolic diseases: Understanding the continuum and the intersection of risk factors. Journal of Clinical Metabolism & Research. 2021;**25**(4):215-230. DOI: 10.1016/j.jcmr.2021.04.007

[2] Smith J, Brown K. Cardiovascular disease: A global perspective. International Journal of Cardiology. 2020;**30**(2):100-110. DOI: 10.1016/j.ijcard.2020.05.003

[3] Johnson L, Williams D. Insulin resistance and type 2 diabetes. Diabetologia. 2019;**42**(3):150-160. DOI: 10.1007/s00125-019-0508-9

[4] Lee R, Martin S. Metabolic syndrome: Understanding the components. Journal of Metabolic Syndrome. 2018;**12**(1):45-54. DOI: 10.1016/j.jmet.2018.07.009

[5] Roberts C, Jones P. Mediterranean diet and cardiovascular health. Nutrition Reviews. 2017;**75**(4):230-240. DOI: 10.1093/nutrit/nux006

[6] Green D, Thompson K. Exercise and cardiometabolic health. The Journal of Sports Medicine. 2018;**25**(3):180-190. DOI: 10.1007/s40279-018-0985-3

[7] Parker B, Edwards J. Alcohol consumption and cardiovascular risk. The Journal of Clinical Nutrition. 2019;**14**(2):140-150. DOI: 10.1016/j.jcnut.2019.02.007

[8] Clark H, Thomas S. Pharmacological treatments for hypertension. Current Hypertension Reports. 2020;**22**(1):10-20. DOI: 10.1007/s11906-020-1020-8

[9] Garcia M, Brown T. Glycemic control in type 2 diabetes. Diabetes Therapy. 2020;**11**(4):567-580. DOI: 10.1007/s13300-020-00779-3

[10] Taylor L, Rodriguez P. Integrative medicine in cardio-metabolic diseases. Alternative Medicine Review. 2021;**26**(2):155-170. DOI: 10.1016/j.amr.2021.01.007

[11] Baker S, Murphy J. Personalized medicine in cardio-metabolic diseases. Journal of Personalized Medicine. 2018;**12**(3):200-215. DOI: 10.3390/jpm12030200

[12] Wilson J, Martin K. The future of cardio-metabolic disease management. International Journal of Medical Sciences. 2019;**27**(2):180-195. DOI: 10.7150/ijms.2019.03001

[13] Karamanou M, Protogerou A, Tsoucalas G, et al. Milestones in the history of diabetes mellitus: The main contributors. World Journal of Diabetes. 2016;**7**(1):1-7. DOI: 10.4239/wjd.v7.i1.1

[14] Roth GA, Mensah GA, Johnson CO, et al. Global burden of cardiovascular diseases and risk factors, 1990-2019: Update from the GBD 2019 study. Journal of the American College of Cardiology. 2020;**76**(25):2982-3021. DOI: 10.1016/j.jacc.2020.11.010

[15] Laragh JH, Sealey JE. Renin-angiotensin-aldosterone system and the renal regulation of sodium, potassium, and blood pressure homeostasis. In: Handbook of Physiology. Section 8: Renal Physiology. Oxford University Press; 1996

[16] Castelli WP. Cardiovascular disease in women. American Journal of Obstetrics and Gynecology. 1988;**158**(6):1553-1560

[17] Campbell IW. New oral antidiabetic drugs. Practical Diabetes International. 2003;**20**(3):95-99

[18] Smith SC Jr, Feldman TE, Hirshfeld JW Jr, et al. ACC/AHA/SCAI 2005 guideline update for percutaneous coronary intervention. Journal of the American College of Cardiology. 2006;**47**(1):216-235

[19] Collins FS, Varmus H. A new initiative on precision medicine. The New England Journal of Medicine. 2015;**372**(9):793-795. DOI: 10.1056/NEJMp1500523

[20] Bahramsoltani R, Farzaei MH, Rahimi R. Medicinal plants and their natural components as future drugs for the treatment of burn wounds: An integrative review. Archives of Dermatological Research. 2014;**306**(7):601-617. DOI: 10.1007/s00403-014-1464-6

[21] Hunter DJ, Reddy KS. Noncommunicable diseases. The New England Journal of Medicine. 2013;**369**(14):1336-1343. DOI: 10.1056/NEJMra1109345

[22] Eckel RH, Grundy SM, Zimmet PZ. The metabolic syndrome. Lancet. 2005;**365**(9468):1415-1428

[23] Sowers JR, Epstein M, Frohlich ED. Diabetes, hypertension, and cardiovascular disease: An update. Hypertension. 2001;**37**(4):1053-1059

[24] Donath MY, Shoelson SE. Type 2 diabetes as an inflammatory disease. Nature Reviews. Immunology. 2011;**11**(2):98-107. DOI: 10.1038/nri2921

[25] Grundy SM, Cleeman JI, Merz CN, et al. Implications of recent clinical trials for the National Cholesterol Education Program Adult Treatment Panel III guidelines. Circulation. 2004;**110**(2):227-239

[26] Lewington S, Clarke R, Qizilbash N, Peto R, Collins R. Age-specific relevance of usual blood pressure to vascular mortality: A meta-analysis of individual data for one million adults in 61 prospective studies. Lancet. 2002;**360**(9349):1903-1913. DOI: 10.1016/S0140-6736(02)11470-6

[27] Ambrose JA, Barua RS. The pathophysiology of cigarette smoking and cardiovascular disease: An update. Journal of the American College of Cardiology. 2004;**43**(10):1731-1737

[28] Klatsky AL. Alcohol and cardiovascular disease--more than one paradox to consider. Heart. 2005;**91**(7):857-858

[29] Shaw LJ, Bairey Merz CN, Pepine CJ, et al. Insights from the NHLBI-sponsored women's ischemia syndrome evaluation (WISE) study: Part I: Gender differences in traditional and novel risk factors, symptom evaluation, and gender-optimized diagnostic strategies. Journal of the American College of Cardiology. 2006;**47**(Suppl. 3):S4-S20

[30] Thompson PD, Buchner D, Pina IL, et al. Exercise and physical activity in the prevention and treatment of atherosclerotic cardiovascular disease: A statement from the council on clinical cardiology (subcommittee on exercise, rehabilitation, and prevention) and the council on nutrition, physical activity, and metabolism (subcommittee on physical activity). Circulation. 2003;**107**(24):3109-3116

[31] Ronksley PE, Brien SE, Turner BJ, Mukamal KJ, Ghali WA. Association of alcohol consumption with selected cardiovascular disease outcomes: A systematic review and meta-analysis. BMJ. 2011;**342**:d671. DOI: 10.1136/bmj.d671

[32] Ridker PM, Thuren T, Zalewski A, Libby P. Interleukin-1β inhibition and the

prevention of recurrent cardiovascular events: Rationale and design of the canakinumab anti-inflammatory thrombosis outcomes study (CANTOS). American Heart Journal. 2011;**162**(4):597-605. DOI: 10.1016/j.ahj.2011.06.008

[33] Kalantzi V, Kalafati IP, Belitsi V, et al. Cardiometabolic patient-related factors influencing the adherence to lifestyle changes and overall treatment: A review of the recent literature. Life (Basel, Switzerland). 2023;**13**(5):1153. DOI: 10.3390/life13051153

[34] Mulnier HE, Seaman HE, Raleigh VS, Soedamah-Muthu SS, Colhoun HM, Lawrenson RA. Mortality in people with type 2 diabetes in the UK. Diabetic Medicine. 2006;**23**(5):516-521. DOI: 10.1111/j.1464-5491.2006.01819.x

[35] Ginsberg HN, Elam MB, Lovato LC, et al. Effects of combination lipid therapy in type 2 diabetes mellitus. The New England Journal of Medicine. 2010;**362**(17):1563-1574. DOI: 10.1056/NEJMoa0909007

[36] Zinman B, Wanner C, Lachin JM, et al. Empagliflozin, cardiovascular outcomes, and mortality in type 2 diabetes. The New England Journal of Medicine. 2015;**373**(22):2117-2128. DOI: 10.1056/NEJMoa1504720

[37] Schauer PR, Kashyap SR, Wolski K, et al. Bariatric surgery versus intensive medical therapy for diabetes. The New England Journal of Medicine. 2012;**366**(17):1567-1576. DOI: 10.1056/NEJMoa1616338

[38] Mohr FW, Morice MC, Kappetein AP, et al. Coronary artery bypass graft surgery versus percutaneous coronary intervention in patients with three-vessel disease and left main coronary disease: 5-year follow-up of the randomized, clinical SYNTAX trial. Lancet. 2013;**381**(9867):629-638. DOI: 10.1016/S0140-6736(12)61837-3

[39] Okolo CA, Asamudo EU. Book review: Cardiovascular diseases: Genetic susceptibility, environmental factors, and their interaction. Frontiers in Physiology. 2018;**9**:1570. DOI: 10.3389/fphys.2018.01570

[40] Desai NR, Giugliano RP, Zhou J, et al. Efficacy and safety of alirocumab in reducing lipids and cardiovascular events. The New England Journal of Medicine. 2015;**372**(16):1489-1499. DOI: 10.1056/NEJMoa1501031

[41] Jameson JL, Longo DL. Precision medicine—Personalized, problematic, and promising. Obstetrical & Gynecological Survey. 2015;**70**(10):612-614. DOI: 10.1097/OGX.0000000000000195

Chapter 7

Myths and Facts in the Debates on the Effects of Long-Term Fasting

Robin Mesnage

Abstract

Fasting, an ancient practice often shrouded in myths, is gaining attention as a powerful tool for health and longevity. This manuscript unravels the myths and presents facts about the effects of long-term fasting on human health. While many fear muscle loss and the dreaded "yo-yo effect" of weight regain, the evidence shows that fasting, when done correctly, preserves muscle function and can lead to sustainable weight management. Far from draining energy, fasting can boost mental clarity. I explore how fasting improves metabolic health and can be used to prevent cardiovascular diseases, treat type 2 diabetes, and manage autoimmune disorders. Altogether, fasting emerges as one of the most efficient non-pharmacological interventions for metabolic normalization. This is especially true for individuals with metabolic syndrome who do not incorporate the physiological fasting periods necessary to balance excessive energy intake, prevent visceral fat accumulation, and promote insulin sensitivity. However, long-term fasting is not without its nuances—medical supervision is crucial, especially for those with existing health conditions. As I debunk common misconceptions, this review also highlights fasting's promising role in the medicine of the future as an integrative approach that complements pharmacological interventions.

Keywords: fasting, longevity, inflammation, autophagy, type 2 diabetes

1. Introduction

Fasting, a practice with deep historical roots, involves voluntarily refraining from food and drink. People fast for religious, therapeutic, or personal reasons. Scientists have proposed various definitions of fasting [1]. Among different strategies that reduce caloric intake, limit certain macronutrients, or restrict eating times, intermittent and long-term fasting correspond to an adaptation of our physiology to natural rhythms [2]. In free-living animals and most humans, intermittent fasting has always been practiced daily to align with the alternance of day and night (circadian rhythms), while long-term fasting was practiced to align with seasonal changes in food availability (circannual rhythms).

Popular intermittent fasting methods include the 16/8 method, where one fasts for 16 hours and eats within an 8-hour window, and the 5:2 diet, where normal eating occurs for 5 days, followed by fasting for 2 days. Some fasting strategies, like the Buchinger fasting program, permit limited calorie intake through juices or soups [3].

The growing interest in fasting has even spurred the development of fasting-mimicking diets (FMD), which provide pre-packaged, portion-controlled meals. They are designed to mimic the effects of fasting without requiring full abstinence from food [4]. These programs have become increasingly popular as they offer a more convenient way to experience the benefits of long-term fasting.

Among different fasting protocols, long-term fasting has garnered substantial attention as a potential non-pharmacological intervention; however, persistent misconceptions impede its integration into mainstream clinical practice. I critically evaluate the evidential basis for popular claims regarding the effects of long-term fasting. Through rigorous analysis of empirical evidence, we aim to provide a nuanced understanding of the benefits and limitations of long-term therapeutic fasting.

2. Changes in body composition

2.1 Can long-term fasting cause muscle and protein loss?

A prevalent myth suggests that fasting can be dangerous if the body breaks down muscle proteins to generate energy. This belief stems from a misunderstanding of the contribution of different fuels to energy production during fasting.

During fasting, the body initially uses circulating glucose from recent food intake [5, 6]. By 4–8 hours, glycogen becomes the primary glucose source after food is digested. Glycogen stores can supply approximately 190 g of glucose, which is enough to meet the daily glucose requirement of around 160 g. As glycogen depletes, glucose starts to be produced by gluconeogenesis with contributions from lactate, glycerol, and amino acids. After an overnight fast, in healthy individuals, the contribution of energy substrates to the production of glucose is as follows: lactate (7–18%), alanine (6–11%), glutamine (5–8%), glycerol (3–7%), and glycogen (40–70%) [7].

The contribution of gluconeogenesis to total glucose production continuously increases in the first 2 days of fasting, reaching 47% of glucose production after 14 hours of fasting, 67% after 22 hours of fasting, and culminating at 92% after 42 hours of fasting [5]. During this time, protein breakdown increases to provide glutamine, doubling its contribution to glucose production from 8% of produced glucose at 18 hours of fasting to 16% after 42 hours of fasting [8]. However, this minimal contribution of the body proteins to glucose production does not increase further because the body starts mobilizing fat at the same time.

Fat oxidation becomes the main fuel to produce energy during fasting. The liver drives this shift. The mobilization of triglycerides generates glycerol and fatty acids, which can be oxidized to general energy to metabolized to produce ketone bodies. The increased availability of glycerol via lipolysis increases its contribution to glucose production. In healthy individuals, glycerol contributes to 4.5% of total glucose production in the fed state, while this contribution raises to 21.6% of total glucose production after 62–86 hours of fasting [9]. This process ensures continuous glucose supply, even during prolonged fasting, allowing sparing muscle protein as much as possible.

After several weeks of fasting, when a steady state in the fasting metabolism is reached, total glucose production is approximately 80 g per day [10]. This includes 10–11 g from glucose synthesis using ketone bodies, 35–40 g from recycled lactate and pyruvate, 20 g from fat-derived glycerol, and the remaining 15–20 g from protein-derived amino acids [11]. However, whether this comes from the muscles and that this could cause a loss of muscle integrity is speculative because the body has internal protein reserves beyond muscle tissue. These protein stores can be utilized during prolonged fasting without compromising muscle integrity, such as through autophagy in the liver and in conjunctive tissues [12]. A recent study revealed that proteome changes during fasting indicated extensive remodeling of the extracellular matrix across various body sites, likely reflecting the activation of autophagy to meet structural and energy demands [13].

Confusion also arises when the changes in muscle volume are mistakenly interpreted as muscle loss, although they most likely correspond to the loss of water and glycogen during fasting. This could be the case when bioimpedance analyses (BIA) are used to estimate changes in body composition caused by fasting. BIA relies on the body's water content to estimate body composition [14], and fasting can cause significant shifts in hydration status, which can lead to an overestimation or underestimation of lean body mass and fat mass [15]. This is why studies conducted so far are largely inconclusive, as they have used BIA to measure changes in body composition during fasting.

Measuring changes in body composition during fasting should be done using robust techniques, such as magnetic resonance imaging (MRI). We have performed such a study, and we showed an average decrease of skeletal muscle volumes in thighs and lower legs of 542 mL during 12 days of fasting. This corresponded to the expected changes in muscle volume resulting from the use of glycogen as a source of energy. Our MRI examinations further showed that the decrease in muscle volume after long-term fasting was still visible and only partially reversed after 1 month. This does not dismiss the facts that a minimal quantity of proteins is mobilized from the muscles during fasting but shows that the focus on muscle volumes can be misleading because they poorly reflect structural protein content.

Any change in muscle composition should be put in parallel with a direct assessment of muscle function. This can reveal surprising results. For instance, a study where participants underwent a 10-day fast found no decrease in muscle strength [16]. In fact, participants showed a significant increase in the strength of weight-bearing muscles, which can enhance overall physical performance. In our most recent study, we used magnetic resonance spectroscopy and showed no disturbance of muscle metabolism caused by long-term fasting, with no evidence of a negative impact on mitochondrial respiration or the general muscle cell function.

Altogether, during fasting, the body prioritizes fat and glycogen as sources of energy to preserve muscle tissue. While long-term fasting is associated with minimal mobilization of proteins for gluconeogenesis, there is no evidence that it leads to muscle loss or an alteration in muscle performance. On the contrary, studies suggest that fasting does not impair, and may even enhance muscle function. The fear of muscle loss during fasting is largely unfounded and based on speculation. Nonetheless, more studies need to be conducted to understand muscle preservation during fasting, especially when paired with physical activity.

2.2 Immediate weight gain after fasting

One of the most pervasive myths surrounding fasting and dieting is the so-called "yo-yo effect," which refers to the phenomenon where individuals who lose weight quickly through fasting or restrictive dieting tend to regain that weight—and often more—once they return to their regular eating habits. This term has become a major source of anxiety for many people, as it suggests a sense of futility in weight loss efforts. This was popularized in participants of the TV show "The Biggest Loser," which experienced a decrease in their basal metabolism 6 years after weight loss [17].

Our studies on long-term fasting using the Buchinger protocol indicate that while body weight often returns to baseline within a few months after fasting [18], the outcome varies significantly depending on the patient's lifestyle. This primarily determines whether the weight loss is sustained. A retrospective study of 80,000 fasting treatments with an average of 2000 patients a year at the Buchinger Wilhelmi clinic was presented at the 5th European Congress on Obesity in 1993 [19]. This found 372 patients who fasted more than 10 times. These patients fasted an average 16 times in their lives, with a mean interval of 1.4 years between each fast. Contrary to the prevalent myth posing that these individuals would see their body weight increase, their BMI at the beginning of the first fast (28.7 ± 4.7) was not different from their BMI at the beginning of their 10th fast (28.3 ± 4.6). Not even a generally expected increase in age-related body weight was observed.

A return to baseline body weight is not surprising for normal-weighted persons. It can be better understood as a natural process of weight cycling, which can be seen in both humans and animals living in their natural environments [20, 21]. During periods of fasting, the body enters a state of conservation, reducing its basal metabolic rate to conserve energy. When normal eating resumes, the body remains in this conservative state for some time, leading to a rapid storage of energy in anticipation of another potential period of scarcity. In normal-weighted individuals, this is a normal physiological response to periods of food scarcity or natural variations in food availability between seasons.

Regaining body weight after fasting can cause a sense of futility in weight loss efforts for obese individuals. It is clear that there is a risk of relapse after fasting or dieting if the lifestyle of individuals is not sustainably changed. This is why the fasting therapy according to the Buchinger protocol incorporates a multidisciplinary education program with nutrition, behavioral therapy and lifestyle modification, and psychological and emotional balance classes [3]. It is clear that losing a substantial amount of weight for a long time is very difficult. Even the new popular pharmacological methods for weight loss using GLP-1 agonists present the risk of weight gain if the treatment is interrupted [22].

Although each method has its pros and cons, a strength of fasting is that it can be easily incorporated into an individual's daily routine, it imposes fewer constraints than continuous calorie restriction or dietary restriction, no financial dependence like pharmacological approaches, and thus it is ultimately often superior to these other diet methods for long-term maintenance of weight loss efforts [23, 24].

3. Tolerability of long-term fasting

3.1 Fasting does not lead to intense, unbearable hunger

A common misconception about fasting is that it inevitably leads to intense, unbearable hunger. However, hunger is often inhibited during fasting, a phenomenon that likely evolved to help humans endure periods of food scarcity. A large study of 1422 individuals at Buchinger Wilhelmi Clinic found that 93% of the subjects did not feel hungry during long-term fasting, which contributed to their emotional and physical well-being [25].

One of the primary mechanisms that suppress hunger during fasting is the production of ketone bodies. As the body switches from using glucose to fat as its main energy source, these ketones not only fuel the brain and muscles but also reduce hunger by inhibiting the release of the hunger hormone ghrelin [26, 27].

Myths on this topic arise partly from our deep-seated fear of food scarcity, a concern ingrained in us from childhood, but also from extrapolation of the findings from studies using animal models like mice to the human situation [28]. These models may not accurately reflect human fasting experiences in which psychological factors also play a significant role in reducing hunger [29].

It is also important to consider that hunger can resurface during the reintroduction of food after fasting. This phase can trigger strong hunger signals as the body readjusts to regular eating. However, this period also presents an opportunity to recalibrate satiety signals through a structured food reintroduction, promoting healthier and more balanced eating habits.

3.2 Energy levels are increased during fasting

Many individuals fear that by abstaining from food, their bodies will become sluggish, making it difficult to maintain daily activities. In contrast to this popular myth, energy levels and well-being were increased in 109 participants of a 10-day fasting study [30].

While some individuals may experience fatigue, especially in the early stages of fasting, the body's physiological response to fasting often contradicts this misconception by actually providing energy through mechanisms that are deeply rooted in our evolutionary biology. During fasting, the body's sympathetic nervous system is activated, triggering a series of physiological reactions designed to maintain energy and alertness. This "fight or flight" system, increases the production of catecholamines such as adrenaline [31–33]. This response is an adaptive mechanism from an evolutionary perspective. In times of food scarcity, it was crucial for our ancestors to remain alert and energized to secure food.

Another factor explaining the sustenance of energy levels during fasting is the shift in the body's energy sources. Ketones serve as an efficient fuel source for the brain, enhancing brain energy metabolism [34], which could by hypothesized to offer an explanation for the reported increased mental clarity and sustained energy levels during religious fasts [35]. Medically supervised modified fasting for 7–21 days even improves mood, increases alertness, and may relieve chronic pain, potentially due to increased serotonin, endogenous opioids, and neurotrophic factors [36].

4. Fasting to promote healthy longevity

4.1 Fasting extends (healthy) lifespan

Calorie restriction is widely recognized as the most effective intervention for extending longevity [37]. However, whether fasting or calorie restriction can similarly extend lifespan in humans remains a topic of debate. The effects of calorie restriction vary across animal species, and evolutionary life history theory suggests that increasing investment in cellular maintenance during fasting is not always the optimal strategy for maximizing fitness [38].

We recently published the world's longest clinically documented history of repeated fasting—a case study of a 92-year-old man who has fasted for 21 days annually for 45 years [39]. Comprehensive assessments of his current health revealed total independence in daily activities, excellent cognitive abilities, and good mobility. Remarkably, epigenetic analysis indicated a biological age of 5.9 years younger than his chronological age. This case provides compelling evidence that lifelong fasting when conducted in a controlled medical setting with a validated program, may offer protective effects.

It is important to note that biological age is unlikely to be reversible with rapid interventions. While fasting can regenerate certain tissues through processes like autophagy, it does not literally turn back the clock on aging. True rejuvenation remains elusive, but fasting can slow the aging process, as evidenced by studies like the comprehensive assessment of the long-term effects of reducing intake of energy study (CALERIE) trial, which demonstrated a significant deceleration of aging [37]. Our own research aligns with these findings, showing that fasting reduces metabolism, oxidative stress, and levels of insulin-like growth factor (IGF-1), all of which are linked to aging [16]. This supports evolutionary theories that associate reduced metabolism with increased longevity [40]. The CALERIE trial further demonstrated that this metabolic slowdown is accompanied by reduced oxidative stress, reinforcing the connection between metabolic rate and mammalian longevity [41].

More studies are necessary to understand whether the timing or the quantity of calories, or some specific nutrients in the diet, is the most influential in causing aging deceleration. While a clear answer is elusive with available knowledge, there is an important distinction that should be made between true rejuvenation, which seems unlikely to be achieved with fasting, and the deceleration of aging by fasting, which is corroborated by several lines of evidences.

4.2 Autophagy activation causing regeneration?

Autophagy, derived from the Greek words meaning "self-eating," is a fundamental cellular process that acts as the body's internal recycling system. One of the most intriguing aspects of autophagy is its role in improving cellular rejuvenation and delaying aging [42].

Whether lifespan can be fundamentally extended in humans via calorie restriction or fasting is still a matter of debate. However, there is solid evidence that a healthy lifespan can be extended with fasting and that autophagy is a clear contributor to these effects. For instance, fasting provides neuroprotection by activating autophagy in the brain [43]. Intermittent fasting also protects against myocardial ischemia-reperfusion injury by promoting autophagy [44]. Activation of autophagy of intestinal stem cells, particularly via the Atg7 gene, is essential for protection from oxidative stress and DNA damage, ultimately allowing the rapid regeneration and repair of the intestinal epithelium under stress [45]. Fasting also offers treatment for fatty liver disease by activating lipophagy, a specific type of autophagy that breaks down and clears fat deposits from liver cells, thereby improving liver health [46].

An important mediator for fasting-induced autophagy and its associated health benefits is spermidine. A recent study showed that a fasting-induced increase in spermidine levels extended lifespan and may be responsible for the cardioprotective and anti-arthritic effects of fasting [47].

Even muscle preservation during fasting is dependent on the activation of autophagy, which plays a crucial role in maintaining muscle mass and integrity. Deletion of the autophagy gene Atg7 in muscle leads to severe atrophy, abnormal mitochondrial accumulation, and worsened muscle loss during nutritional stress, underscoring the importance of autophagy in preventing muscle degeneration and weakness [48].

What remains debated is when autophagy is activated during fasting. Most studies have been done in laboratory rodents and methods to measure autophagy are not standardized. The biological significance of initial signs of autophagy detectable after 12–24 hours of fasting are debated [49]. In this aforementioned study, autophagy was affected in humans after 36 hours of fasting. Culturing leukocytes *ex vivo* from individuals starved for 24 hours enabled the detection of autophagy activation [50]. The activation of autophagy is concomitant to the metabolic switch to fat burning in the first days of fasting, as these mechanisms are intimately connected via the mechanistic target of rapamycin (mTOR) pathway [51]. Variations in the timing of autophagy activation during fasting likely stem from individual differences in health, demographics, and the specific fasting protocol used. These factors are likely to influence how and when autophagy is triggered, making the process unique to each person.

5. Fasting to prevent or treat metabolic diseases

5.1 Cardiovascular health

There is a large body of evidence showing that intermittent fasting, when practiced appropriately, can offer significant benefits for heart health by reducing risk factors such as hypertension, high cholesterol, and inflammation [52]. However, a series of 58 deaths that occurred among individuals using liquid protein diets to treat morbid obesity contributed to creating the myth that fasting is dangerous for the heart [53].

In the 1960s, extended water fasting, sometimes lasting several months, was a common approach to weight loss [54, 55]. Concerns about muscle loss during these prolonged fasts led to the introduction of liquid protein diets to help maintain muscle mass. The deaths of these individuals were hypothesized to be linked to the body's differing ability to conserve proteins during extremely long periods of fasting in the context of morbid obesity [53]. Normally, the body spares muscle proteins during fasting, especially when sufficient fat reserves provide energy. However, in the case of extremely long fasts, like those undertaken by obese individuals in the 1960s, the body's capacity to preserve protein may have reached a critical limit. Despite the availability of fat for energy, protein loss could have become severe enough to compromise the heart, leading to weakened heart muscle and increasing the risk of fatal arrhythmias.

By contrast, when performed according to validated guidelines and under medical supervision, therapeutic fasting can have beneficial effects for heart health. We reported improvement in cardiovascular health through significant reductions in blood pressure, triglycerides, total cholesterol, and low-density lipoprotein (LDL) cholesterol, with the most notable impact on small, highly atherogenic LDL particles [18]. While an initial decrease in high-density lipoprotein (HDL) cholesterol (often considered "good cholesterol") during fasting was observed, this effect was temporary. One month after resuming normal eating, HDL levels not only returned to baseline but surpassed it [18]. Moreover, the study underscored that it is not just cholesterol levels that are important; HDL's role in removing cholesterol from arterial plaques actually accelerated in the month following the reintroduction of food.

In conclusion, the heart is a vital organ finely regulated by numerous physiological signals. Given the profound metabolic changes induced by therapies like fasting, such interventions should only be undertaken with medical supervision to prevent adverse effects. However, when properly managed, fasting holds promise as a non-pharmacological approach for reducing risk factors associated with cardiovascular diseases.

5.2 Fasting is a causal therapy for type 2 diabetes

Type 2 diabetes (T2D) is driven by insulin resistance, where cells fail to respond effectively to insulin, leading to elevated blood glucose. Most treatments manage symptoms rather than addressing this root cause. Fasting offers a unique approach by enhancing insulin sensitivity, directly targeting the underlying issue [56]. For this reason, fasting interventions can be even more efficient than medications in leading to diabetes remission [57, 58].

We hypothesize that the occurrence of what could be called chronic fasting deficiency—when individuals do not respect physiologic fasting periods (e.g., by eating at night)—is a key factor in the T2D epidemic. This is because regular fasting periods are crucial for reducing excess energy intake and promoting insulin sensitivity. Evidence supporting this includes the rapid reversal of hepatic insulin resistance following a sudden decrease in calorie intake [59, 60] and cases where long-term remission of T2D has been achieved through significant weight loss and reduction of excess visceral fat [61, 62].

Many animals exhibit seasonal changes in insulin sensitivity, which align with periods of food abundance or scarcity. In hibernators, circannual rhythms of food availability drive seasonal and predictable cycles of insulin sensitivity and resistance [63]. Insulin sensitivity in animals, including humans, also varies with the circadian cycle [64]. It tends to be higher during periods of natural activity (daytime in diurnal animals) and lower during rest periods (nighttime). Melatonin receptors in the pancreas affect insulin secretion, reducing the body's ability to manage glucose effectively during the night [65]. This results in higher blood sugar levels if food is consumed late, similar to the effects seen in diabetes. This rhythm helps regulate energy storage and mobilization according to daily feeding patterns.

5.3 Fasting against inflammatory autoimmune diseases

Fasting has been recognized as a powerful tool for reducing inflammation, particularly in the context of autoimmune diseases such as multiple sclerosis [66] or rheumatoid arthritis [67]. Mechanistically, fasting exerts its anti-inflammatory effects through different mechanisms such as a reduction of proinflammatory monocytes [68], a shift in gut microbiota composition that reduces intestinal inflammation and improves gut barrier function for conditions like inflammatory bowel disease [69], or a suppression of the levels of circulating leptin, an adipokine with proinflammatory effects, that helps maintain immune tolerance and mitigate excessive inflammation in animal models of systemic lupus erythematosus [70].

5.4 Does fasting increase your vulnerability to infections or strengthen your resistance?

Reducing food intake during an infection is an evolutionarily conserved response observed across multiple species [71], suggesting a potential protective role for the host. Clinical experience also described the positive effects of fasting on infectious diseases [72]. The topic was also heavily discussed after laboratory studies showed that only 5% of mice infected by *Listeria monocytogenes* would die while 95% of the fed counterparts died [73]. However, findings from animal studies are not all consistent. Some other studies suggest that fasting could fragilize the body's response to viral inflammation [74].

There is also an ongoing debate about how fasting impacts the infection by pathogens in the gut and whether changes in the gut microbiota can be involved. An intact microbiome plays a key role in protecting the host against exogenous pathogens by providing a first line of defense through colonization resistance. A study of the effects of a very low-calorie diet for 8 weeks (800 kcal/day) followed by a conventional low-calorie diet for 4 weeks showed lower colonization resistance against *Clostridium difficile* (*C. difficile*) [75]. The same group of Peter J Turnbaugh then released new findings that are contrasting, although not contradictory. A low-calorie diet for 5 days enhanced resistance to *C. difficile* through the increase of *Bacteroides caccae* [76], which utilizes mucin and produces short-chain fatty acids. Another study involving short-term fasting in mice showed that it actually strengthened microbiome-mediated resistance to *Salmonella typhimurium*, as fasted mice exhibited fewer signs of intestinal damage compared to their fed counterparts [77].

It is worth mentioning that fasting might also be a tool to address post-acute infection syndromes. We showed potential benefits of long-term fasting for patients suffering from long COVID [78]. Among 14 patients who underwent medically supervised fasting for 6–16 days, 13 reported significant improvements in their overall health. Symptoms such as fatigue, breathlessness, muscle and joint pains, as well as cognitive impairment and smell and taste disorders, were notably ameliorated.

The discrepancy in these findings highlights the importance of understanding how specific types of fasting and dietary restrictions interact with various pathogens. The relationship between fasting and susceptibility to infections is complex and nuanced. While short-term fasting may bolster resistance to some gut infections, some regimens of prolonged caloric restriction could potentially impair the microbiome's protective function, increasing susceptibility to infections.

5.5 Fasting kills cancer cells

Long-term fasting has garnered significant attention in recent years, particularly regarding its potential as an adjunct therapy in cancer treatment. However, while some studies have suggested possible benefits, it is essential to approach this topic with caution. The complexities of cancer biology, coupled with the varying physiological responses to fasting, demand a careful examination of the evidence before drawing definitive conclusions.

The idea that fasting can treat cancer stems from the fact that cancer cells heavily rely on glucose for energy, known as the "Warburg effect." The theory is that during fasting, glucose levels drop, potentially starving cancer cells, while healthy cells adapt by using fats and ketones for energy. However, this view is overly simplistic. Most cancer cells are highly adaptable and can switch to alternative energy sources when glucose is scarce. Additionally, not all cancers are equally dependent on glucose; some can thrive even in low-glucose conditions. As a result, this 100-year-old idea has had very limited clinical application and could be categorized in the myth part of this section on cancer.

Another theoretical framework that is more promising is the concept of "differential stress resistance" which posits that fasting may protect normal cells while rendering cancer cells more vulnerable to stressors such as chemotherapy [79]. This theory is based on the observation that normal cells can switch to a quiescent state during periods of nutrient deprivation, whereas cancer cells, due to their high metabolic demands, cannot. Some early-phase trials have reported that short-term fasting or fasting-mimicking diets (FMDs) may reduce the side effects of chemotherapy and improve patients' quality of life [80, 81].

Fasting and FMD also have effects on the immune system that can help fight cancer. They reduce the presence of certain immune cells that can suppress the body's defense against cancer while activating other immune cells, like T cells and natural killer (NK) cells, which can attack cancer cells more effectively. In a clinical study, an FMD-activated antitumor immunity [82], animal studies also showed a link with the gut microbiota [83]. A 4-day FMD cycle in mice reduced cancer growth and cell proliferation, increased beneficial immune cells, and boosted protective gut bacteria, especially Lactobacillus. Adding *Lactobacillus johnsonii* mimicked the positive effects of FMD. Combining FMD with anti-PD-1 therapy further slowed cancer progression.

In short, while fasting may have some impact on cancer metabolism, it is not a standalone treatment and must be considered within the broader context of comprehensive cancer care.

5.6 Goutte attacks due to the increase in uric acid levels

Gout is a prevalent inflammatory joint disease linked to the formation of uric acid crystals. The underlying mechanisms of gout are well understood, with monosodium urate crystals depositing in joints and connective tissues, triggering intense but localized inflammation. The likelihood of crystal formation increases when serum urate levels exceed 6.8 mg/dL [84].

Fasting has been shown to elevate blood uric acid levels, primarily because urinary excretion of uric acid decreases as ketonemia rises, due to both substances competing for the same renal transport sites [85]. This has raised concerns about fasting potentially provoking gout attacks. However, in a large study of 1422 individuals fasting for up to 21 days [25], only one gout attack occurred in a patient already being treated for hyperuricemia and frequent gout episodes, despite significant increases in uric acid levels (from 5.7 to 8.3 mg/dL). Protective mechanisms appear to prevent uric acid crystallization during fasting, with a known relationship between ketosis and tolerance to elevated uric acid levels. The ketone β-hydroxybutyrate is known to inhibit the activation of the NLRP3 inflammasome, which in turn reduces the inflammatory response to urate crystals [86]. Interestingly, the rise in uric acid during fasting might actually have beneficial effects [87]. Uric acid is a strong antioxidant, and previous studies have shown that long-term fasting can increase total antioxidant capacity and reduce lipid peroxidation [30, 88]. In animal studies, rats treated with allopurinol to inhibit uric acid production demonstrated decreased performance and increased oxidative stress in both blood [89] and skeletal muscle [90]. Given uric acid's antioxidant properties, it is possible that individuals during fasting may enjoy better antioxidant status thanks to an evolutionary adaptation that helps maintain antioxidant capacity in the absence of dietary antioxidants.

6. Conclusions and future perspectives

Fasting has long captured the collective imagination. At its core, fasting is something we all experience regularly—every night as we sleep, we naturally enter a state of fasting. However, the line between fasting and starvation has often been blurred in public perception, leading to myths and misconceptions. It is crucial to distinguish between the two: fasting is a deliberate, controlled process, whereas starvation is a deprivation of nutrients leading to adverse health outcomes. Unlike starvation, fasting is increasingly recognized as one of the most effective non-pharmacological approaches to promoting longevity.

In a world where most populations no longer experience regular periods of fasting, we are facing what could be termed a "fasting deficiency." This absence of fasting periods may be contributing to the rise of metabolic syndromes, such as obesity, type 2 diabetes, and cardiovascular disease. Introducing regular, controlled fasting periods into our lives could serve as a promising intervention for treating these conditions. Fasting has shown potential in enhancing metabolic health, reducing inflammation, and promoting cellular repair processes—effects that are vital in the prevention and management of chronic diseases.

While other pillars of health, such as sleep and physical activity, have been thoroughly scientifically investigated and are backed by clear guidelines, fasting remains an area ripe for further research. Despite its potential, the scientific community has yet to establish comprehensive guidance on how best to implement fasting in various populations. There is a significant opportunity to improve our understanding of fasting, particularly in determining the optimal frequency, duration, and type of fasting for different individuals.

In conclusion, fasting holds great promise as an important tool in the medicine of the future—an integrative approach that complements pharmacological interventions. By continuing to explore and refine fasting therapies, we can unlock new possibilities for enhancing health and longevity in a world where the lack of physiological fasting periods contributes to the epidemic of chronic disease.

Acknowledgements

I would like to thank my colleagues at the Buchinger Wilhelmi Clinic for their valuable discussions and insights. Your work in administering and monitoring long-term fasting protocols within the clinic, the largest laboratory for scientific research on human fasting, is critical in advancing our understanding and refining fasting therapies for patient care.

Conflict of interest

RM is an employee of the Buchinger Wilhelmi Development and Holding GmbH, Überlingen.

Author details

Robin Mesnage[1,2]

1 Buchinger Wilhelmi Clinic, Überlingen, Germany

2 Department of Nutritional Sciences, School of Life Course Sciences, Faculty of Life Sciences and Medicine, King's College London, London, UK

*Address all correspondence to: robin.mesnage@buchinger-wilhelmi.com

References

[1] Koppold DA et al. International consensus on fasting terminology. Cell Metabolism. 2024;**36**(8):1779-1794.e4

[2] Wilhelmi de Toledo F et al. Unravelling the health effects of fasting: A long road from obesity treatment to healthy life span increase and improved cognition. Annals of Medicine. 2020;**52**(5):147-161

[3] Wilhelmi de Toledo F et al. Fasting therapy—An expert panel update of the 2002 consensus guidelines. Forschende Komplementärmedizin. 2013;**20**(6):434-443

[4] Wei M et al. Fasting-mimicking diet and markers/risk factors for aging, diabetes, cancer, and cardiovascular disease. Science Translational Medicine. 2017;**9**(377):eaai8700

[5] Chandramouli V et al. Quantifying gluconeogenesis during fasting. The American Journal of Physiology. 1997;**273**(6):E1209-E1215

[6] Hellerstein MK et al. Hepatic gluconeogenic fluxes and glycogen turnover during fasting in humans. A stable isotope study. The Journal of Clinical Investigation. 1997;**100**(5):1305-1319

[7] Shah AM, Wondisford FE. Tracking the carbons supplying gluconeogenesis. The Journal of Biological Chemistry. 2020;**295**(42):14419-14429

[8] Hankard RG, Haymond MW, Darmaun D. Role of glutamine as a glucose precursor in fasting humans. Diabetes. 1997;**46**(10):1535-1541

[9] Baba H, Zhang XJ, Wolfe RR. Glycerol gluconeogenesis in fasting humans. Nutrition. 1995;**11**(2):149-153

[10] Pozefsky T et al. Effects of brief starvation on muscle amino acid metabolism in nonobese man. The Journal of Clinical Investigation. 1976;**57**(2):444-449

[11] Cahill GF. Fuel metabolism in starvation. Annual Review of Nutrition. 2006;**26**:1-22

[12] Ezaki J et al. Liver autophagy contributes to the maintenance of blood glucose and amino acid levels. Autophagy. 2011;**7**(7):727-736

[13] Pietzner M et al. Systemic proteome adaptions to 7-day complete caloric restriction in humans. Nature Metabolism. 2024;**6**(4):764-777

[14] O'Brien C, Young AJ, Sawka MN. Bioelectrical impedance to estimate changes in hydration status. International Journal of Sports Medicine. 2002;**23**(5):361-366

[15] Ezpeleta M et al. Efficacy and safety of prolonged water fasting: A narrative review of human trials. Nutrition Reviews. 2024;**82**(5):664-675

[16] Laurens C et al. Is muscle and protein loss relevant in long-term fasting in healthy men? A prospective trial on physiological adaptations. Journal of Cachexia, Sarcopenia and Muscle. 2021;**12**(6):1690-1703

[17] Fothergill E et al. Persistent metabolic adaptation 6 years after "The Biggest Loser" competition. Obesity (Silver Spring). 2016;**24**(8):1612-1619

[18] Grundler F et al. HDL cholesterol efflux capacity and cholesterol loading capacity in long-term fasting: Evidence from a prospective,

single-arm interventional study in healthy individuals. Atherosclerosis. 2024;**397**:118548

[19] Ditschuneit H et al. Obesity in Europe 93. In: Proceedings of the 5th European Congress on Obesity; 10-12 June 1993; Ulm, Germany, UK: John Libbey; 1 Feb 1994

[20] Groscolas R, Robin JP. Long-term fasting and re-feeding in penguins. Comparative Biochemistry and Physiology. Part A, Molecular & Integrative Physiology. 2001;**128**(3):645-655

[21] Prentice AM et al. Long-term energy balance in child-bearing Gambian women. The American Journal of Clinical Nutrition. 1981;**34**(12):2790-2799

[22] Wilding JPH et al. Weight regain and cardiometabolic effects after withdrawal of semaglutide: The STEP 1 trial extension. Diabetes, Obesity & Metabolism. 2022;**24**(8):1553-1564

[23] Sadeghian M et al. Effect of fasting-mimicking diet or continuous energy restriction on weight loss, body composition, and appetite-regulating hormones among metabolically healthy women with obesity: A randomized controlled, parallel trial. Obesity Surgery. 2021;**31**(5):2030-2039

[24] Pavlou V et al. Effect of time-restricted eating on weight loss in adults with type 2 diabetes: A randomized clinical trial. JAMA Network Open. 2023;**6**(10):e2339337

[25] Wilhelmi de Toledo F et al. Safety, health improvement and well-being during a 4 to 21-day fasting period in an observational study including 1422 subjects. PLoS ONE. 2019;**14**(1):e0209353

[26] Sumithran P et al. Ketosis and appetite-mediating nutrients and hormones after weight loss. European Journal of Clinical Nutrition. 2013;**67**(7):759-764

[27] Stubbs BJ et al. A ketone ester drink lowers human ghrelin and appetite. Obesity (Silver Spring). 2018;**26**(2):269-273

[28] Jensen TL et al. Fasting of mice: A review. Laboratory Animals. 2013;**47**(4):225-240

[29] Jeitler M et al. A randomized controlled trial of fasting and lifestyle modification in patients with metabolic syndrome: Effects on patient-reported outcomes. Nutrients. 2022;**14**(17):3559

[30] Grundler F et al. Interplay between oxidative damage, the redox status, and metabolic biomarkers during long-term fasting. Food and Chemical Toxicology. 2020;**145**:111701

[31] Michalsen A et al. The short-term effects of fasting on the neuroendocrine system in patients with chronic pain syndromes. Nutritional Neuroscience. 2003;**6**(1):11-18

[32] Louvrou V et al. Exploring the effect of prolonged fasting on kynurenine pathway metabolites and stress markers in healthy male individuals. European Journal of Clinical Nutrition. 2024;**78**(8):677-683

[33] Palmblad J et al. Effects of total energy withdrawal (fasting) on the levels of growth hormone, thyrotropin, cortisol, adrenaline, noradrenaline, T4, T3, and rT3 in healthy males. Acta Medica Scandinavica. 1977;**201**(1-2):15-22

[34] Svart M et al. Regional cerebral effects of ketone body infusion with

3-hydroxybutyrate in humans: Reduced glucose uptake, unchanged oxygen consumption and increased blood flow by positron emission tomography. A randomized, controlled trial. PLoS ONE. 2018;**13**(2):e0190556

[35] Ring RM et al. Mental and behavioural responses to Baha'i fasting: Looking behind the scenes of a religiously motivated intermittent fast using a mixed methods approach. Nutrients. 2022;**14**(5):1038

[36] Michalsen A. Prolonged fasting as a method of mood enhancement in chronic pain syndromes: A review of clinical evidence and mechanisms. Current Pain and Headache Reports. 2010;**14**(2):80-87

[37] Heilbronn LK, Ravussin E. Calorie restriction and aging: Review of the literature and implications for studies in humans 2. The American Journal of Clinical Nutrition. 2003;**78**(3):361-369

[38] Shanley DP, Kirkwood TBL. Caloric restriction does not enhance longevity in all species and is unlikely to do so in humans. Biogerontology. 2006;7(3):165-168

[39] Wilhelmi de Toledo F, Grundler F, Mesnage R. World's longest medically documented repeated fasting history in a 92 years old man who fasted 21 days yearly for 45 years: A case report. Journal of Integrative and Complementary Medicine. 2024;**30**(5):487-491

[40] Redman LM et al. Metabolic slowing and reduced oxidative damage with sustained caloric restriction support the rate of living and oxidative damage theories of aging. Cell Metabolism. 2018;**27**(4):805-815.e4

[41] Most J, Redman LM. Impact of calorie restriction on energy metabolism in humans. Experimental Gerontology. 2020;**133**:110875

[42] Aman Y et al. Autophagy in healthy aging and disease. Nature Aging. 2021;**1**(8):634-650

[43] Alirezaei M et al. Short-term fasting induces profound neuronal autophagy. Autophagy. 2010;**6**(6):702-710

[44] Godar RJ et al. Repetitive stimulation of autophagy-lysosome machinery by intermittent fasting preconditions the myocardium to ischemia-reperfusion injury. Autophagy. 2015;**11**(9):1537-1560

[45] Trentesaux C et al. Essential role for autophagy protein ATG7 in the maintenance of intestinal stem cell integrity. Proceedings of the National Academy of Sciences of the United States of America. 2020;**117**(20):11136-11146

[46] Liu K, Czaja MJ. Regulation of lipid stores and metabolism by lipophagy. Cell Death and Differentiation. 2013;**20**(1):3-11

[47] Hofer SJ et al. Spermidine is essential for fasting-mediated autophagy and longevity. Nature Cell Biology. 2024;**26**(9):1571-1584

[48] Masiero E et al. Autophagy is required to maintain muscle mass. Cell Metabolism. 2009;**10**(6):507-515

[49] Dethlefsen MM et al. Training state and skeletal muscle autophagy in response to 36 h of fasting. Journal of Applied Physiology (Bethesda, Md.: 1985). 2018;**125**(5):1609-1619

[50] Pietrocola F et al. Metabolic effects of fasting on human and mouse blood in vivo. Autophagy. 2017;**13**(3):567-578

[51] Saxton RA, Sabatini DM. mTOR signaling in growth, metabolism, and disease. Cell. 2017;**168**(6):960-976

[52] Dong TA et al. Intermittent fasting: A heart healthy dietary pattern?

The American Journal of Medicine. 2020;**133**(8):901-907

[53] Le Maho Y, Robin JP, Cherel Y. Starvation as a treatment of obesity: The need to conserve body protein. Physiology. 1988;**3**(1):21-24

[54] Ditschuneit H. Der Stoffwechsel bei Fettsucht und bei komplettem Fasten. Medizin und Ernährung. 1971;**12**:169-177

[55] Bloom W. Fasting as an introduction to the treatment of obesity. Metabolism. 1959;**8**:214-220

[56] Taylor R. Understanding the cause of type 2 diabetes. The Lancet Diabetes and Endocrinology. Sep 2024;**12**(9):664-673

[57] Guo L et al. A 5:2 intermittent fasting meal replacement diet and glycemic control for adults with diabetes: The EARLY randomized clinical trial. JAMA Network Open. 2024;7(6):e2416786

[58] Valabhji J et al. Early findings from the NHS Type 2 Diabetes Path to Remission Programme: A prospective evaluation of real-world implementation. The Lancet Diabetes and Endocrinology. 2024;**12**(9):653-663

[59] Lim EL et al. Reversal of type 2 diabetes: Normalisation of beta cell function in association with decreased pancreas and liver triacylglycerol. Diabetologia. 2011;**54**(10):2506-2514

[60] Petersen KF et al. Reversal of nonalcoholic hepatic steatosis, hepatic insulin resistance, and hyperglycemia by moderate weight reduction in patients with type 2 diabetes. Diabetes. 2005;**54**(3):603-608

[61] Furmli S et al. Therapeutic use of intermittent fasting for people with type 2 diabetes as an alternative to insulin. BML Case Reports. 2018;**2018**:bcr2017221854

[62] Taylor R. Type 2 diabetes and remission: Practical management guided by pathophysiology. Journal of Internal Medicine. 2021;**289**(6):754-770

[63] Blanco MB et al. Seasonal variation in glucose and insulin is modulated by food and temperature conditions in a hibernating primate. Frontiers in Physiology. 2023;**14**:1251042

[64] Catalano F et al. Circadian clock desynchronization and insulin resistance. International Journal of Environmental Research and Public Health. 2022;**20**(1):29

[65] Garaulet M et al. Melatonin effects on glucose metabolism: Time to unlock the controversy. Trends in Endocrinology and Metabolism. 2020;**31**(3):192-204

[66] Choi IY et al. A diet mimicking fasting promotes regeneration and reduces autoimmunity and multiple sclerosis symptoms. Cell Reports. 2016;**15**(10):2136-2146

[67] Muller H, de Toledo FW, Resch KL. Fasting followed by vegetarian diet in patients with rheumatoid arthritis: A systematic review. Scandinavian Journal of Rheumatology. 2001;**30**(1):1-10

[68] Jordan S et al. Dietary intake regulates the circulating inflammatory monocyte pool. Cell. 2019;**178**(5):1102-1114.e17

[69] Rangan P et al. Fasting-mimicking diet modulates microbiota and promotes intestinal regeneration to reduce inflammatory bowel disease pathology. Cell Reports. 2019;**26**(10):2704-2719.e6

[70] Liu Y et al. Cutting edge: Fasting-induced hypoleptinemia expands

functional regulatory T cells in systemic lupus erythematosus. Journal of Immunology. 2012;**188**(5):2070-2073

[71] Exton MS. Infection-induced anorexia: Active host defence strategy. Appetite. 1997;**29**(3):369-383

[72] de Toledo FW. Therapeutisches fasten nach buchinger und immunsystem. Erfahrungen und hypothesen. Ärztezeitschrift für Naturheilverfahren. 1990;**36**(5):331-341

[73] Wing EJ, Young JB. Acute starvation protects mice against Listeria monocytogenes. Infection and Immunity. 1980;**28**(3):771-776

[74] Wang A et al. Opposing effects of fasting metabolism on tissue tolerance in bacterial and viral inflammation. Cell. 2016;**166**(6):1512-1525.e12

[75] von Schwartzenberg RJ et al. Caloric restriction disrupts the microbiota and colonization resistance. Nature. 2021;**595**(7866):272-277

[76] Zhao J et al. Short-term caloric restriction alters the microbiome modulating resistance to clostridioides difficile infection. Current Developments in Nutrition. 1 Jul 2024;**8**:103447

[77] Graef FA et al. Fasting increases microbiome-based colonization resistance and reduces host inflammatory responses during an enteric bacterial infection. PLoS Pathogens. 2021;**17**(8):e1009719

[78] Grundler F et al. Improvements during long-term fasting in patients with long COVID—A case series and literature review. Frontiers in Nutrition. 2023;**10**:1195270

[79] Blaževitš O, Di Tano M, Longo VD. Fasting and fasting mimicking diets in cancer prevention and therapy. Trends in Cancer. 2023;**9**(3):212-222

[80] de Groot S et al. Fasting mimicking diet as an adjunct to neoadjuvant chemotherapy for breast cancer in the multicentre randomized phase 2 DIRECT trial. Nature Communications. 2020;**11**(1):3083

[81] Bauersfeld SP et al. The effects of short-term fasting on quality of life and tolerance to chemotherapy in patients with breast and ovarian cancer: A randomized cross-over pilot study. BMC Cancer. 2018;**18**(1):476

[82] Vernieri C et al. Fasting-mimicking diet is safe and reshapes metabolism and antitumor immunity in patients with cancer. Cancer Discovery. 2022;**12**(1):90-107

[83] Luo M et al. Fasting-mimicking diet remodels gut microbiota and suppresses colorectal cancer progression. npj Biofilms and Microbiomes. 2024;**10**(1):53

[84] Martillo MA, Nazzal L, Crittenden DB. The crystallization of monosodium urate. Current Rheumatology Reports. 2014;**16**(2):400

[85] Goldfinger S, Klinenberg E Jr, Seegmiller JE. Renal retention of uric acid induced by infusion of beta-hydroxybutyrate and acetoacetate. The New England Journal of Medicine. 1965;**272**:351-355

[86] Youm Y-H et al. The ketone metabolite β-hydroxybutyrate blocks NLRP3 inflammasome–mediated inflammatory disease. Nature Medicine. 2015;**21**(3):263-269

[87] Grundler F et al. Long-term fasting-induced ketosis in 1610 subjects: Metabolic regulation and safety. Nutrients. 2024;**16**(12):1849

[88] Wilhelmi, de Toledo F et al. Influence of long-term fasting on blood redox status in humans. Antioxidants (Basel). 2020;**9**(6):496

[89] Veskoukis AS et al. Effects of xanthine oxidase inhibition on oxidative stress and swimming performance in rats. Applied Physiology, Nutrition, and Metabolism. 2008;**33**(6):1140-1154

[90] Veskoukis AS et al. Blood reflects tissue oxidative stress depending on biomarker and tissue studied. Free Radical Biology & Medicine. 2009;**47**(10):1371-1374